10633950

ONE HUNDRED YEARS
OF THOMISM

Holy Transfiguration Monastery

The Monks of Mt. Tabor
(Byzantine-Ukrainian Catholic)

17001 Tomki Rd., Redwood Valley, CA 95470
(707) 485-8959

ONE HUNDRED YEARS OF THOMISM

Aeterni Patris and Afterwards
A Symposium

Edited By
Victor B. Brezik, C.S.B.

CENTER FOR THOMISTIC STUDIES
University of St. Thomas
Houston, Texas 77006

NIHIL OBSTAT:
Reverend James K. Farge, C.S.B.
Censor Deputatus

IMPRIMATUR:
Most Reverend John L. Morkovsky, S.T.D.

Bishop of Galveston-Houston
January 6, 1981

First Printing: April 1981

Copyright © 1981 by The Center For Thomistic Studies

All rights reserved. No part of this book may be used or
reproduced in any manner whatsoever without written
permission, except in the case of brief quotations embodied
in critical articles and reviews. For information, write to The
Center For Thomistic Studies, 3812 Montrose Boulevard,
Houston, Texas 77006.

Library of Congress catalog card number: 80-70377

ISBN 0-9605456-0-3

Printed in the United States of America

Contents

Introduction

Many things can happen during the span of a hundred years. Empires can rise and fall, economies can change, cultural values can be replaced. Modes of production, of transportation, of communication can also be altered, as can technology and scientific theory as well. Even religious and philosophic perspectives can become radically modified, all within a single century.

The past one hundred years has witnessed shifts and transformations in all these areas. Names like Hitler, Mussolini, Stalin, Roosevelt and Churchill in practical politics; Freud, Jung and Adler in psychology; Einstein, Bohr and Heisenberg in physics; Alexander Graham Bell, Thomas Edison and Marconi in electronic communications; Henry Ford in earth travel, the Wright brothers in air travel, and John Glenn and Neil Armstrong in space-travel; John L. Lewis and Philip Murray in labor relations; Bergson, Dewey, Husserl, Heidegger and Wittgenstein in philosophy; Popes John XXIII and Paul VI in religion, are all associated with historical change. Such names and numerous others only remind us that the past century has been a busy one and that we are not living in the same human world that people inhabited a hundred years ago.

It is amidst such historical and cultural vicissitudes that must be traced that philosophical movement of the past century which has received the name of *Thomism*. Without debating here the merits of the name, *Thomism* in a restricted sense, since St. Thomas was primarily a theologian, stands for that emphatic formulation of Christian philosophy which derives its inspiration from the teaching of St. Thomas Aquinas.

1

Christian Philosophy, particularly in the form of Thomism, was given a strong impetus a century ago when Pope Leo XIII issued his influential Encyclical letter *Aeterni Patris*. The exact date was August 4, 1879. In time, the impact accelerated the incipient Thomist renaissance of the nineteenth century into a veritable movement of studies, critical editions and publications mounting like a mighty crescendo which turned Thomism into a leading philosophy of the day. One need only mention undertakings like the Leonine Commission for the publication of a critical edition of the writings of St. Thomas Aquinas, centers of Thomistic studies such as The Higher Institute of Philosophy at Louvain, the Dominican school of Saulchoir in France, the groups of French and Belgian Jesuits inspired by St. Thomas, the Pontifical Institute of Mediaeval Studies, and names of scholars like Mercier, Grabmann, Gilson, Maritain and a host of others, as well as the pervasion of Thomism in numerous Catholic institutions of learning throughout the world, to realize the immense growth of interest in and adherence to the doctrine of St. Thomas that eventually resulted from the firm recommendation made in *Aeterni Patris* one hundred years ago.

The centenary year of *Aeterni Patris*, however, leaves many questions seeking answers. Can one still speak of an on-going Thomistic movement today or has the movement come to a halt? What happened to the Thomistic movement around the time of Vatican Council II and afterwards, and why did it happen? Is the apparent decline of interest in Thomism a laudable and welcome event or is it a deplorable loss? What are the prospects of a revival of interest in the doctrine of St. Thomas and how viable would be an effort to rejuvenate a serious study of the philosophical dimensions of his teaching as an acceptable outlook for the present time?

These and similar questions were on the mind of Professor Anton C. Pegis when he took up his duties as the original Director of the development of a Center for Thomistic Studies which would sponsor a graduate program in philosophy at the University of St. Thomas. Such questions, he thought, needed to be explored and it seemed that the appropriate format for discussing them would be a symposium at which prominent Thomist scholars would have an occasion to address themselves to them. The occurrence of the centenary of the Encyclical *Aeterni Patris* on the eve, as it were, of the scheduled opening of the graduate philosophy program in the fall of 1980, provided an additional purpose and incentive for holding such a symposium. After the death of Professor Pegis on May 13, 1978, Professor Vernon J. Bourke of St. Louis University succeeded to the position of Director of the Center for Thomistic Studies and undertook to carry out the plans for the symposium.

The general plan of the Symposium comprises both a retrospect and a prospect together with a look at the present condition of Christian Philosophy. The symposium papers clearly reflect this general plan. The papers of Leonard Boyle, James Weisheipl, Armand Maurer and Donald Gallagher are in retrospect. The present situation of Thomism and of Christian Philosophy is considered in the two position papers of Ralph McInerny and Michael Bertram Crowe and the lecture of Robert Henle on *Transcendental Thomism.* Leo Sweeney and Joseph Owens addressed their papers to the question of the prospects of Thomism. Vernon Bourke's dinner address outlines the aims and purposes of the graduate program in philosophy and the Center for Thomistic Studies.

Regrettably, space does not permit the inclusion of the illuminating and insightful remarks of the panelists participating in the two Round Table discussions during the Symposium, nor the questions addressed to the speakers from the audience and their replies. Nevertheless, I wish to acknowledge here the contribution made to the success of the Symposium by the distinguished panelists, included among whom were Edward A. Synan of the Pontifical Institute of Mediaeval Studies, James H. Robb of Marquette University, Frederick D. Wilhelmsen of the University of Dallas, Sister Mary T. Clark of Manhattanville College, Ronald D. Lawler of The Catholic University of America, and Marianne M. Childress of St. Louis University.

While not all the questions that could be asked about Christian Philosophy and Thomism are answered in the following pages, it is hoped that collectively the papers of this Symposium do comprise an informative assessment of the present situation both of Christian Philosophy and of Thomism. Certainly they should complement the commemorative studies on St. Thomas made in 1974 in honor of the 700th anniversary of his death and also the papers of other symposia celebrating the centenary of *Aeterni Patris*.

Victor B. Brezik, C.S.B.
Center For Thomistic Studies
University of St. Thomas

Looking At
The Past

A Remembrance Of Pope Leo XIII: The Encyclical *Aeterni Patris*

Leonard E. Boyle, O.P.

Pontifical Institute of Mediaeval Studies

A hundred years ago these two months past, on 4 August 1879, and just eighteen months after he had become pope as Leo XIII, Joachim Pecci, lately bishop of Perugia for some thirty-two years, published an encyclical *Aeterni Patris* on, to use his own title, "The restoration in Catholic schools of Christian philosophy according to the mind of St. Thomas Aquinas, the Angelic Doctor."[1]

Opening this encyclical with the reminder that "the only-begotten Son of the Eternal Father...had commanded the Apostles to go and teach all nations" (Matt. 28:19), and that this same Son had set up the Church he had founded as "the common and only teacher of all peoples," Leo said that the supreme pastors or popes had always been on guard to see that "human disciplines and especially that of philosophy were taught according to the rule of the Catholic faith."

Philosophy, he said, was most important because a right approach to all other sciences depended upon it. If one were to look around and seek for a cause of present disorders, and of the bad attitude to divine and human things that was prevalent, this would be found in the "schools of philosophers." The first way, of course, to combat these

7

errors was by the light of faith, but human reason was not to be despised on that account. Philosophy, and the deployment of reason in the service of faith, had a long and honorable place in the history of Christian tradition, from the Fathers of the Church to the recent Vatican Council. Indeed, "a perpetual and plentiful use of philosophy is necessary, so that sacred theology may acquire and take on the nature, habit and character of a true science." As Augustine and others have pointed out, and in practice attempted to do, the very mysteries of faith can be made clearer, so far as is humanly possible, by the use of reason and philosophy.

Of course, Pope Leo went on, we are aware that many extol reason in an inordinate fashion, but this does not mean that philosophy, when it is guided by and obedient to faith, cannot be a powerful instrument against error and disorder. For although reason itself can err, faith, as the recent Vatican Council says, frees reason from, and protects it against, the incursions of error.

If one looks at the history of philosophy, the great role of philosophy in the service of faith stands out clearly. There are the Fathers of the Church who go by the name of Apologists, there are Irenaeus, Clement of Alexandria, Origen, Tertullian, Anastasius, Lactantius, Basil, Augustine, Boethius, John Damascene, Anselm, and there are the great Doctors, called Scholastics, of the Middle Ages, whose genius was finely described by Pope Sixtus V in his bull *Triumphantis* of 1588, where he speaks of the power of scholastic theology and of the achievement of the two most glorious representatives of that Scholastic age, the Angelic St. Thomas and the Seraphic St. Bonaventure.

Of all these scholastic doctors, Pope Leo now said, "the prince and master of all by far is Thomas Aquinas," for Thomas "gathered together, encompassed and surpassed the teaching of all the other doctors, providing a singular source of defense to the Catholic Church." There is no part of philosophy of which he did not treat solidly and lucidly. What is more, he nicely distinguished reason and faith, yet brought the two together as friends. He clearly set out the rights of each, yet to each he gave its full dignity. He raised reason so high that it hardly could be on a higher pinnacle, but at the same time he provided faith with an array of rational arguments which hardly could be bettered.

What Thomas achieved, the pope went on, has been acknowledged far and wide. Leaving aside for obvious reasons the Dominicans, whose glory Thomas is, it is noteworthy how many founders of religious orders or legislators require the teaching of Thomas of their subjects, the Benedictines, for example, the Carmelites, the Augustinians, the Jesuits. In the many celebrated academies and schools which once flourished in Europe—Paris, Salamanca, Douai, Toulouse, Louvain, Padua, Bologna, Naples, Coimbra, to mention only a few—in these "great centers of human wisdom," Thomas reigned supreme. Predecessor after predecessor of mine, Leo continued, praised Thomas and urged teachers and students to follow his teaching. Ecumenical Councils such as Lyons II, Vienne, Florence, and the recent Vatican Council, always held him in honor, and particularly the great Council of Trent, which in a mark of respect never afforded any other Catholic Doctor, "placed the *Summa* of St. Thomas on the altar of the Council with the Scriptures and the Decretals."

It is, then, Pope Leo said sorrowfully, a great shame that in spite of all of these acts of recognition, Thomas is no longer honored as he once was. Much of this is due, he suggested, to innovators of the sixteenth century who, placing reason on a higher plane than faith, opened the way to a multiplicity of discordant opinions, and eventually to doubt about everything. Worse still, all of this worked its way into the teaching of Catholics too. Pushing the old wisdom aside, many took to new currents of thought. Instead of building on what was there already, they attempted to construct anew on what was in fact a shifting foundation.

All was not darkness, however, Leo was glad to note. Not a few philosophers and, indeed, a goodly number of bishops, have labored and are laboring to restore the teaching of Thomas to its rightful place in a hope of rejuvenating philosophy in the church at large.

I, in my turn, the pope concluded, urge all of you patriarchs, primates, archbishops and bishops whom I am addressing in this encyclical letter, to do your very best to restore, and to promote the restoration of, "the golden wisdom of St. Thomas."

Such a restoration, the pope was sure, would make for "the safeguarding and integrity of the Catholic faith, and the betterment of all sciences." First of all, in these turbulent days of ours when the Christian faith is being attacked by the machinations and fallacies of something which passes for wisdom, young men, and young clerics in particular, have need of a strong and robust doctrine of the type that Thomas offers. Then there are those who place all their trust in reason alone and hate all that is held dear by Christianity: for these, nothing (grace always excepted) is more to the point than the solid teaching of the Fathers and the Scholastics, deploying reason as it does to such effect. Finally, the mess that civil society and family life are in all around, should profit hugely from "the teaching of the volumes of Thomas." There people will find a full and proper consideration of that "liberty" which today is fast turning into license. There they will learn about the divine origin of any and every authority, about laws and the force of law, about the fatherly and just rule of the popes, about obedience to higher authority, about mutual love among all. There in Thomas will be found a great and unambiguous teaching to help overthrow those principles of a new dispensation which are so pernicious to public well-being and the fixed order of things. There the physical sciences, which are so much in favor at present, and the natural sciences, to which Thomas and particularly Albert the Great devoted much time, will find help to enable them to reach to the principles underlying new discoveries and new patterns of things.

This famous encyclical took the world of learning, within and without the Catholic church, by surprise. There had been nothing like it before in the history of the church. Popes had praised Thomas and recommended him. Councils had consulted, cited and accepted him. But at no point, not even in the pontificates of the Dominican Popes Pius V and Benedict XIII, had any pope attempted to put Thomas on the pedestal on which Leo XIII now placed him, and to the exclusion, seemingly, of all others.

Nothing in the pontificates of Leo's predecessors since the French Revolution gave any inkling of what was to come. The papacy indeed felt keenly the depredations of indifferentism, rationalism, traditionalism, and ontologism in those beleaguered years, and resoundingly condemned one or other of these and similar movements in 1824, 1832, 1835, 1844, 1846, 1855, 1857, 1860, 1862, 1863, and all of them together in the Syllabus of Errors in 1864.[2] Yet while the various popes from Leo XII in 1824 to Pius IX in 1864 took umbrage at attacks both from the right (traditionalism) and the left (rationalism) on the Scholastic method, they never went beyond stating, as Pius IX did in 1855, that "doctors such as Thomas and Bonaventure" were not to be pilloried for their seeming rationalism, or, as Pius IX again did in 1863, that the method of "the old school" and its "chief doctors" was not to be scorned as outworn if not outmoded.[3]

Yet, for all this, there should not have been any great

surprise at this stunning move of Leo XIII. He was not an unknown when elected in 1878, nor was his Thomism an overnight conversion. He had been, in fact, the popular candidate for the papacy for some years, mainly because of the stature he had achieved in his diocese of Perugia, where he had been bishop since 1846 and a cardinal since 1853. From 1860—ten years before the fall of Rome to the troops of the Risorgimento—Perugia and the part of the Papal States in which it stood had been occupied by the forces of Victor Emmanuel II, and Leo, then Joachim Pecci, while not giving an inch on ecclesiastical liberties, had emerged as a peacemaker and as a man who could adapt with dignity to a new situation.[4]

At Perugia, too, from the first days of his episcopate in 1846, he had made no secret of his devotion to and intense interest in St. Thomas and his thought. He was a young man then, just turned thirty-six, and, as well, a legate in early and somewhat forced retirement, who for three years and more had served as Nuncio at Brussels, and had seen at first-hand what was happening in industrial nations such as Belgium, and had observed the social problems afflicting cities which he had visited such as Paris, Cologne and London. At Brussels he had become a friend of the Italian priest and patriot, and inventor of "Ontologism," Vincenzo Gioberti, then in exile. At Louvain he had witnessed all too closely and unwisely, and at the cost seemingly of his Nunciature, the tensions between the Jesuits of Namur and the "liberal" University of Louvain, where Gioberti, Ubaghs and others taught to much excitement. He was scarcely settled in his new charge at Perugia in 1846 when he took steps to arm his clergy against the dangers inherent, as he saw it, in the various philosophies in vogue in Catholic intellectual centers such as Louvain, particularly in Ontologism, which in reaction to the sceptical trend of post-Kantian speculation, asserted that the idea of Being, which is the first and simplest of all, is an immediate perception of Absolute Being, that God Himself is the guarantee of the validity of human ideas, and that all human knowledge implies an immediate intuition of uncreated truth. Pecci therefore reorganized his seminary at Perugia at once, threw out the current and pervasive Cartesian manuals of philosophy, and introduced manuals of Thomistic inspiration. All teaching, Bishop Pecci insisted, should be based on St. Thomas. The *Summa* should be studied, article by article, then what Thomas had to say should be applied to modern problems. To lend some backbone to the changes, he called in his brother Joseph Pecci, now an ex-Jesuit. Joseph, in fact, took over all of philosophy, taught it there for nearly fifteen years, and as Cardinal Pecci in 1879, probably had as much a hand as his brother the pope in the formulation of *Aeterni Patris*.[5]

The quiet revolution effected by the Pecci brothers at Perugia from 1846 onwards was almost in isolation when it began. Although teaching in seminaries and Catholic colleges could be classed as "scholastic" or even "neoscholastic," it was largely of a Suarezian persuasion in theology and of a Cartesian in philosophy. Thomas, his *Summa* and his teaching in general were not at all in favor, and had not been for quite a long time—a fact which often comes as a shock to the many today who imagine that there never had been a time when Thomas was not taught and revered. At the beginning of the nineteenth century, indeed, Thomas was caught between two fires. On the one hand, the heirs of the rationalist and idealist philosophies which had swept Europe since the days of Descartes in the seventeenth century looked upon Thomas and the whole of Scholasticism as utterly irrelevant. On the other, the traditionalists of varying hues who were trying to make good the ravages of the French Revolution which, in their

Holy Transfiguration Monastery

The Monks of Mt. Tabor
(Byzantine-Ukrainian Catholic)

17001 Tomki Rd., Redwood Valley, CA 95470
(707) 485-8959

opinion, these philosophies had brought about, found the Scholastics, and Thomas above all, far too rationalist in their approach for safety and stability.[6]

Thomas, of course, had always been studied and respected in his own Dominican Order from the days of his canonization in the early fourteenth century. In the centuries after the Reformation, however, that assiduous study of Thomas and his thought had hardly any impact outside the Dominicans themselves. Their *studia generalia* tended more and more to be detached from university centers and universities, and ceased to be the open *studia* which they were by custom and certainly had been for most of the Middle Ages. In any case, in the years immediately after the French Revolution the Dominican Order was in no position to act as flag-bearer of a Thomistic revival. In Austria and Germany it was barely ticking over. In Italy, England and Ireland it was crippled and poor. In France, where once it had had Thomist stalwarts such as Gonet, Goudin and Billuart, it had disappeared altogether, though it would be resurrected in the 1840s by Lacordaire. In Spain, where in fact the Dominicans were detached from the rest of the Order from 1804 to 1870, it was living on a memory of the glories of Melchior Cano, Domingo Báñez and the rest, or was sparring tiresomely with the Molinists.

The Dominicans, in a word, were in disarray, and it was only at the General Chapter of 1838 in Rome—a chapter attended by representatives from the ten Italian provinces, Malta, England, Ireland and the United States—that something was done to reestablish the old *ratio studiorum* of pre-Revolution days, when in the 1760s and 1770s there had been a notable attempt by the General Tommaso de Boxadors to spur the Order on to an even greater fidelity than before to St. Thomas. At Rome in 1838 de Boxadors' great circular letter of 1757 on Thomistic studies was invoked, a three-year course of philosophy was set up based on the manual (1777-1783) of his collaborator Salvatore Roselli, and a five-year study of the *Summa* of St. Thomas was made obligatory on all candidates for degrees.

The Chapter bore fruit, at least in that various printings of Thomas' works were sponsored or supported by the Order, notably the well-known Parma *Opera omnia* of 1852-1873, and in that the old and hallowed *Studium generale* at the Minerva convent in Rome was refurbished, and had a leading Thomistic light in the 1870s in Tommaso Zigliara and his celebrated *Summa philosophica* of 1876. In the dissident Spanish branch of the Order, too, steps were taken in 1832 to implement de Boxadors' directive of 1757, and there the Order soon produced men of the quality of Ceferino Gonzales, who with Zigliara and Joseph Pecci would be one of the 'Thomist' Cardinals of Leo XIII. He produced an influential *Philosophia elementaris* in 1868, and in 1873, a year before he became bishop of Málaga, founded the first explicitly Thomist journal, the *Ciencia tomista*.[7]

However, the feeling of the Pecci brothers of Perugia for Thomas and, in effect, the roots of *Aeterni patris*, go well back beyond this Dominican reawakening and to days indeed when the Order was still dormant and dislocated. What the Pecci brothers were about in Perugia from 1846 onwards was in fact one of the first concrete achievements of a non-Dominican neo-Thomist movement which had begun some forty or fifty years earlier at Piacenza in the north of Italy, and which had an effect on the Pecci brothers through some disciples of a certain Canon Vincenzo Buzzeti (1778-1824).

Buzzetti, who was born in 1778, studied first until 1798 at what is now generally recognized as the cradle of the neo-Thomist movement, the Vincentian "Alberoni" College in Piacenza, where the manuals of philosophy in use were not the usual Cartesian ones but those of the Dominicans Roselli and Goudin. In 1798 he moved to the former Jesuit College of S. Pietro, where he came under the influence of two ex-Jesuit Suarezian Thomists, the Spaniards José and Balthazar Masdeu. When that college was suppressed by the French in 1806, he joined the staff of the new diocesan seminary.[8]

Vincenzo Buzzetti, however, might never have had the posthumous fame he has enjoyed were it not for the fact that while teaching the *Summa* of St. Thomas at the seminary in Perugia in 1810, two of his students were the brothers Serafino and Domenico Sordi who, indirectly, were to pass on the torch of Buzzetti's Thomism to the Pecci brothers. For when the Jesuit Order, suppressed since 1773, was restored by Pius VII in 1814, these two Sordi brothers joined it, bringing with them some of Buzzetti's enthusiasm for Thomas.

With Serafino Sordi in the Jesuit novitiate and scholasticate was the young and later very distinguished Luigi Taparelli d'Azeglio (1793-1862), on whom some of Serafino's Thomistic spirit began to rub, albeit slowly. In 1824, the year, as it happens, of Buzzetti's death, the Collegio Romano or Gregorian University as it is known today, was handed back to the Jesuits, and Taparelli became its first director. By the following year Taparelli seems to have been won over finally to full Thomism, and since the teaching of St. Thomas was prescribed by the Jesuit constitutions, the young director felt strongly that the Collegio Romano should lead the way. But the generality of the professors, more interested in Suárez and Descartes than Aristotle and Thomas, laughed at what they called the "soporific Aristotelian jargon" of Thomas, with the result that Taparelli had to be content with a quasi-secret society of fellow-enthusiasts who met quietly in one another's rooms and studied hand-written notes put together by

Serafino Sordi, Buzzetti's old pupil.[9]

What is not without interest for the history of Leo XIII and *Aeterni Patris* is that one of the original 400 students in that first year of the Collegio Romano, the year, too, in which his brother Joseph joined the Jesuits, was Joachim Pecci. He was only fourteen at the time, but he was a brilliant student of literature and science, and a prize-winner on many occasions. He was too young, of course, to belong to the "Peripatetics," as Taparelli's Thomistic circle was dubbed by those who did not share his views, but he was close enough to Taparelli to be his student-assistant in philosophy and to teach the "repeat" classes at the Collegio Germanico in his behalf. Clearly he must have caught some of the Taparelli enthusiasm for Thomas, too, for in a letter in November 1828 to his brother Charles, he asked him to send on a copy of the *Summa* of St. Thomas which he knew to be in their library at Carpineto, the home of this Pecci family of minor nobility.[10]

Because of his Thomism, Taparelli was moved from the Collegio Romano to Naples in 1829, where as Provincial of the Jesuits, and with the support of Domenico Sordi, an even more forthright and "political" Thomist than his brother Serafino, the Thomist circle was reconstituted, only to fall to pieces in 1833 when, at the behest of the "absolutist" regime of the Bourbons of Naples, Taparelli was exiled to Sicily and Domenico Sordi was forbidden to teach any more, and in particular to teach anything to do with the natural law and the divine or any other right of kings.

By this time Joachim Pecci was a nuncio in Benevento and Joseph a young Jesuit priest far removed from his brother. But when as bishop and professor they joined forces at Perugia some thirteen years later, they were in a splendid position to do openly for Thomas and his teaching what Luigi Taparelli d'Azeglio and the Sordi brothers had been prevented from accomplishing even secretly at the Collegio Romano and Naples. Thirty years were to pass before they extended the Perugia experiment to the church at large.

From their Thomistic outpost in Perugia, the Pecci brothers must have been heartened as, from 1850 onwards, Thomas and his teaching seemed to be coming more and more into their own. In Rome the new and powerful if semi-official papal journal *Civiltà cattolica*, with Jesuits from the old Collegio Romano and Naples enclaves in charge of or supporting it—Serafino Sordi, Luigi Taparelli, Curci and Liberatore—came out firmly and unequivocally on the side of Thomism in 1853, and remained at war for the next twenty-five years or more with the entrenched non-Thomists, Suarezians and Cartesians of the Collegio Romano or Gregorian University. Soon the Dominicans at the Minerva began to be more perky and visible, too, with Zigliara the leading light, but it was not until 1909, and long after *Aeterni Patris*, that the Dominicans as a whole attempted to emulate the Gregorian and to set up an open and international establishment. At Rome, as well, the German Jesuit Joseph Kleutgen wrote three influential volumes on the problems of God and of religious knowledge in his *Theologie der Vorzeit* between 1853 and 1870, and three more on *Philosophie der Vorzeit* from 1860-1863. At the seminary in Naples, canon Gaetano Sanseverino (1811-1865), a recent convert from Cartesianism, produced in 1862 a *Philosophia Christiana cum antiqua et nova comparata* of which the Pecci brothers thought very highly. At Bologna, the egregious Jesuit Cornoldi, researching deeply into relations between reason and faith, launched a review *La scienza italiana* and founded a remarkable Accademia filosofico-medica di S. Tommaso d'Aquino.[11]

At best, however, these were the efforts of individuals,

and there was little or no rapport between the tiny pockets of neo-Thomism, whether in Italy or Spain, Paris, Louvain or Vienna, to mention a few of the more prominent. The chief Roman bastion of learning, the Gregorian, was still as unbreachable as it had been in Taparelli's day in the 1820s. Even the Papacy was dragging its heels, and a petition by the Pecci brothers in 1875 to have St. Thomas declared patron of Catholic schools fell on deaf ears.

Three years later the fortunes of seemingly unwanted neo-Thomism underwent a swift, sharp change. In his very first encyclical, *Inscrutabili Dei*, a short two months after his election as Leo XIII, Joachim Pecci of Perugia underlined the importance of philosophy and especially of the doctrine of St. Thomas for the Christian reconstruction of society and of Catholic culture. Shortly afterwards, he commissioned the Cardinal-Vicar of Rome to organize a philosophical academy at the Roman seminary of S. Apollinare, and put his brother Joseph on the committee. One who had an audience of Leo at the time wrote to Montalembert in France that Leo had insisted during it on the enduring character of the thought of Thomas in contrast to the transitory nature of that of Gioberti, Rosmini and the like.[12] Just as he had done at Perugia thirty-two years before, Leo in that first summer of 1878 ordered that only the philosophy of St. Thomas was to be taught in the Roman seminary, and that the Cartesian manual then in use, that of Bonelli, was to be replaced by either Signoriello's abridgement of Sanseverino's *Philosophia christiana* or the *Summa* of Zigliara. In the autumn he installed Kleutgen at the Gregorian, and at an audience granted to the professors of that university in November, said very pointedly that "true ecclesiastical science, coming from the Fathers of the Church, had been systematized by the Scholastic doctors and especially by Thomas Aquinas." His was a philosophy he wished to restore, he said, and

his was a teaching which the Jesuit constitutions prescribed—a prescription that was, he had no need to remind
them, all important for the Gregorian, "where religious
and seminarians from all over the world were being
formed philosophically and theologically."

The Gregorian professors, many of whom were forced
to leave after the encyclical on St. Thomas was issued, paid
no attention to Leo's words, and in the six or seven
months before *Aeterni Patris* appeared, the pope, at the
suggestion of his brother, set up open sessions on
Thomistic philosophy for all students of Roman colleges.

The Jesuits at the Gregorian were inordinately slow to
understand what was in the wind, but to a shrewd ob-
server such as the French ambassador there was no mis-
taking the signs. Commenting on the appointment of
Joseph Pecci and Tommaso Zigliara as cardinals in the following May, three months or so before the encyclical, he
said of the Dominican Zigliara, "His title to the distinction
which has just been conferred on him rests on the conformity of his opinions with those of the Holy Father on
scholastic questions according to the method of St.
Thomas Aquinas. The pope is very anxious to give a great
push to that teaching of Aquinas and has it in mind to
consecrate a special encyclical to a fresh affirmation of
Thomistic thought."[14]

The question, however, of just what was in Leo's mind
when he, his brother Joseph and Matteo Liberatore of the
Civiltà cattolica first drafted *Aeterni Patris* in the Spring of
1879 is still very much an open one. Was he, as some
maintain, wholly oblivious to the vibrant pluralism of the
medieval Scholastics when he exalted St. Thomas, "the
archimandrite of theologians," as he termed him in that
letter of 1828 to his brother Charles, above them all? Was
he, as his wholesale condemnation in 1887 of the teachings
of Rosmini has suggested to others, totally preoccupied

with counteracting the influence of that Ontologism and its cognates which he had first seen at close quarters at Louvain more than forty years before when he struck up a friendship with its originator Gioberti? And remembering his passage on "obedience to higher authority" and on the "fatherly and just rule of the popes," was he, as still others darkly suspect,[15] plainly haunted by the blow to papal power and prestige that had resulted from the loss to the papacy of Perugia, his own diocese, of Rome, the very capital of Christendom, of the whole Papal States, the expression of that Temporal Power which had seemed to be part and parcel of the papacy? Or, finally, was he, as Gilson thought, just "a supreme philosopher"[16] who loved St. Thomas, or, as young Dominican students used to be told, was he simply bowled over by Zigliara, whose lectures at the Minerva (or so the Dominican story goes), he used to follow from behind a curtain?

These are questions, however silly on the whole, which can only be answered in all their implications when the files on *Aeterni Patris* in the Vatican Archives have been examined. Happily, this is now possible, since one of the first acts of the present Pope John Paul II was to declare the Vatican Archives open for the whole of Leo's pontificate.

Although I suspect that one or two historians I know are already packing their bags and polishing their magnifying glasses, it might not be a bad beginning for an institute such as this here in Houston which is being inaugurated now on this first centenary of *Aeterni Patris*, to "corner" those files, set some young philosopher-historian to work on them, and once for all, and, needless to say, *iuxta mentem sancti Thomae*, ferret out the truth, come what may.

1. The encyclical *Aeterni Patris* does not have such a title, but a year later, in the encyclical *Cum hoc sit* of 4 August 1880 which declared St. Thomas patron of studies in Catholic schools, Leo XIII himself provided the title given above when he wrote, 'idonea ad rem opportunitas accessit ab Encyclicis litteris Nostris De philosophia christiana ad mentem S. Thomae Aquinatis Doctoris

Angelici in scholis catholicis instauranda, quas superiori anno hoc ipso die publicavimus.' The text of *Aeterni Patris* is in *Acta Apostolicae Sedis* 12 (1878-1879): 97-115, that of *Cum hoc sit* is ibid. 13 (1879-1880): 56-59.

2. H. Denzinger, *Enchiridion Symbolorum*, 32nd ed. by A. Schönmetzer (Barcelona and Freiburg-im-Breisgau 1963), nn. 2720 (1824), 2730-2732 (1832), 2738-2740 (1835), 2765-2769 (1844), 2775-2777 (1846), 2812-2814 (1855), 2828-2831 (1857), 2835-2839 (1860), 2850-2861 (1862), 2865-2867 (1863), 2901-2980 (*Syllabus*, 1864).

3. Ibid., nn. 2814, 2876.

4. In general on Leo XIII see E. Sodorini, *Leone XIII*, 2 vols. (Milan, 1932), and the useful but undocumented essay of R. Quardt, *The Master Diplomat*, trans. I. Wolston (Staten Island, 1964).

5. He was appointed to the Sapienza in Rome in 1861.

6. E. Hocedez, *Histoire de la Théologie au XIXe siècle*, I (Paris, 1948): 104-130, 151-175, etc.

7. A. Walz, 'Il tomismo dal 1800 al 1879,' *Angelicum* 20 (1943): 300-326.

8. See G.F. Rossi, La filosofia nel Collegio Alberoni e il Neotomismo (Piacenza, 1959), *Il movimento neotomista piacentino iniziato al Collegio Alberoni da Francesco Gerussi nel 1751 e la formazione di Vincenzo Buzzetti* (Vatican City, Biblioteca per la storia del Tomismo 4, 1974).

9. R. Jacquin, *Taparelli* (Paris, 1943), pp. 51-55, etc. C.M. Curci, *Memorie del Padre Curci* (Florence, 1891), pp. 62-65.

10. J.-B. Boyer d'Agen, *La jeunesse de Léon XIII* (Tours, 1896), p. 244; and for Leo XIII at the Collegio Romano, C. de T'Serclaes, *Le pape Léon XIII, Sa vie, son action religieuse, politique et sociale*, I (Bruges, 1894): 36-43.

11. The bibliography on the revival is vast, but good basic information is to be found in A. Masnovo, *Il neo-tomismo in Italia* (Milan, 1923); P. Dezza, *I neotomisti italiani del XIX secolo*, 2 vols. (Milan, 1942, 1944); A. Piolanti, *Pio IX e la rinascita del Tomismo* (Vatican City, Biblioteca per la storia del Tomismo 2, 1974).

12. R. Aubert, *Aspects divers du néo-thomisme sous le pontificat de Léon XIII* (Rome, 1961), p. 25.

13. Ibid., p. 32.

14. Ibid., p. 45.

15. P. Thibault, "Savoir et pouvoir." *Philosophie thomiste et politique cléricale au XIXe siècle* (Quebec, 1972), pp. 199-208, etc.

16. E. Gilson, *La philosophie et la théologie* (Paris, 1960), p. 235: 'Léon XIII prend place dans l'histoire de l'Eglise comme le plus grand philosophe chrétien du XIXe siècle et l'un des plus grands de tous les temps.'

Commentary

James A. Weisheipl, O.P.

Pontifical Institute of Mediaeval Studies

A commentator on a major inaugural paper such as this must necessarily be brief and largely laudatory. The latter comes very easily, and I have only two brief points to make. *First*, Fr. Boyle has presented with the utmost clarity, as only he can, the essential message of Pope Leo XIII in his first major encyclical *Aeterni Patris*, promulgated 100 years ago last August 4th. And he has outlined the main elements that led to its publication, particularly in Italy and in the life of Gioacchino Pecci himself. But it is of utmost importance that each one here read and digest the message of Leo's *Aeterni Patris* in its entirety, possibly during these days of the Symposium. It is also essential that one appreciate as fully as possible the entire background of this charter of the neo-Thomistic revival, particularly as seen in the life and times of Pio IX, whose pontifical archives have been opened and magnificently studied since 1903. *Second*, I must confess that I myself was polishing my magnifying glass in Oxford (but for other purposes) when I read of Pope John Paul's decision to open the Vatican Archives for the whole of Leo's pontificate. I can only support Fr. Boyle's suggestion that this Center for Thomistic Studies in Houston give as much priority as possible to "cornering" at least this part of those archives. Now at long last we shall perhaps know who had a hand in the various drafts and suggestions for this masterpiece of Leo XIII. I had always known (on circumstantial evidence) that

23

Cardinal Joseph Pecci, Cardinal Zigliara, and Josef Kleutgen were in the running, although the ultimate responsibility and authority always rested with Leo XIII himself.
But not until reading Fr. Boyle's paper did I imagine that
Matteo Liberatore, S.J., was even listed to run.

A commentator, unfortunately, is paid not only to laud
and endorse what the main speaker has said so elegantly;
he has also to prod, and stimulate reflection. Again I shall
be brief. But this time in three points:

1) It is important to note that the encyclical *Aeterni Patris*
itself has no title or even subtitle. The title attributed by Fr.
Boyle to Leo himself, namely, "The restoration in Catholic
schools of Christian philosophy according to the mind of
St. Thomas Aquinas, the Angelic Doctor," is in no official
publication of the document, and the phrase *philosophia
Christiana* is nowhere to be found in the entire text (as
Gilson himself acknowledged). That editors and trans-
lators immediately appended some such title is not at all
surprising, since French Catholics had been calling for a
philosophie chrétienne since the 1840s; San Severino, *Civiltà
cattolica* and other Italian Thomists had made the term
Filosofia Cristiana popular since the early 1850s; and even
Franz Ehrle, commenting at length on *Aeterni Patris* in
Stimmen aus Maria Laach immediately after its promulga-
tion, related it to "die Restauration der christlichen Philosophie." It is still uncertain which editor or translator first
appended any such subtitle, particularly with the phrase
"Christian philosophy." The only reason I raise this in-
significant point is because of the inordinate significance
the phrase assumed in the idle debates of the 1920s and
'30s, which involved just about all the leading Thomists in
Europe in those decades and later.

2) The history of Thomism certainly still has not been
written, least of all its history in the past 100 years. We are
still too close to it. We used to say, in my Oxford days, that

a subject cannot really be studied objectively until it has been dead at least 100 years. Certainly a beginning must be made; and already numerous partial attempts have been made in print, often with a recognizable bias. I suggest, however, that no solid foundation can be laid without comprehending the ideological errors that beset the whole pontificate of Pius IX, notably as he saw them in the religious fervor of Giovanni Mazzini of Genoa (c.1805-1872), and condemned in the Syllabus of Errors in 1864. I am not suggesting that Mazzini was in any way an original thinker. Far from it. But he embodied in a most extraordinary way the fanatical *Zeitgeist* of all non-Catholic thinkers that (as Leo XIII saw it) came "under the influence of the Reformers of the 16th century," and that led to "the multiplication of philosophical systems beyond all reason." The two basic principles of Mazzini's *Credo* were simply: the inevitability of Human Progress, and the so-called "Principles of '89," i.e., *Liberté, Egalité et Fraternité*. The important thing is the way Mazzini understood the principles of his *Credo* that faced Pius IX and even Leo XIII as he wrote *Aeterni Patris*. Personally, I do not think that Leo XIII would have been in the least dissuaded by the pluralism of medieval scholasticism. He knew what he wanted. And he wanted the restoration of the philosophy of St. Thomas Aquinas, especially as it is to be found in the *Summa theologiae*, thoroughly understood and applied to modern problems. The fact that Leo's ambitious program has never been universally implemented, but only here and there, was in no way due to Leo's ignorance of medieval pluralism, concern for the papal states lost, or any failure to do everything in his own power during his pontificate.

3) Finally, it may come as no surprise that Leo's *Aeterni Patris* was received by a surprised world with mixed feelings. Leaving aside European reaction, which I have not

studied, American Catholic reaction was terribly divided
and bewildered. While the *Catholic Telegraph* of Cincinnati,
the *Catholic Vindicator* of Milwaukee, the *Catholic Mirror* of
Baltimore printed a translation of the full text, and the
Boston Pilot printed a long dispatch on its first page explaining the encyclical—all within a few weeks of its pro-
mulgation—there just were not enough American professors in Catholic seminaries and colleges capable of comply-
ing with it. While less than a handful of writers expressed
their enthusiasm in 1879 and 1880 for *Aeterni Patris* as a
touchstone for solving modern problems, the great majority of Catholic and non-Catholic intellectuals expressed
grave scepticism, doubts, and misgivings about the relevance of St. Thomas to modern philosophy, scientific
discoveries, social and economic problems of free enterprise, democracy, and even the place of religion in the
modern world of politics separating church and state.
While the encyclical *Rerum novarum* (1891) evoked the
greatest Catholic response in the U.S., the biggest obstacle
to *Aeterni Patris* always remained the triumph of modern
science, the presumed warfare between religion and
science (e.g., John H. Draper's book of 1873, Andrew
Dixson White's notorious history of 1896, etc.), and the
inability of Thomists to face the problems of natural
science without escaping into metaphysical principles.
Even Fr. Edward A. Pace of Catholic University, probably
the American best prepared to employ St. Thomas as a
touchstone for science in the last decade of the nineteenth
century (because of his Roman doctorate in Thomistic
philosophy and Leipzig doctorate in experimental psychology under Wilhelm Wundt) recessed into "Thomas the
metaphysician" to resolve problems of the psychological
unity of man. The most heated scientific problem of the
day was, of course, the evolutionary theories of Darwin,
Huxley, and Spencer. Even the Bavarian Fr. John

Gmeiner, originally the most sympathetic Thomist cosmologist then teaching at St. Thomas Seminary in St. Paul, eventually gave up his attempt to accommodate Darwinian evolution to St. Thomas' *rationes seminales*, and ended by advising "that the only safe refuge for [Thomas' cosmological theories of matter and form, and the rest of his science] seems to be the sublime and misty heights of metaphysical abstraction." (*Modern Sc. Views*, 1884, p. 16).

So, the net result of various attempts has been to relegate selected ideas of Thomistic natural philosophy to "metaphysics," and accept the latest view of modern science whatever it happened to be. It took a non-Thomist, Alfred North Whitehead many years later, to recognize what he called "the fallacy of misplaced concreteness" inherent in all post Cartesian science prior to relativity. In the field of Thomistic natural philosophy the field is still wide open to all the hopes of *Aeterni Patris*. Whether these hopes can still be realized to the advancement of science and humanity depends upon us.

The Legacy of Etienne Gilson

Armand A. Maurer, C.S.B.

Pontifical Institute of Mediaeval Studies

Speaking of the legacy of Etienne Gilson, the first thing that should be said is the impossibility of doing justice to the subject in the time at my disposal. He has left us a rich and varied heritage in philosophy, theology, education, literature and politics. Only a voluminous book, like the forthcoming biography by Father Laurence Shook, could give an adequate account of his long and full life and our indebtedness to it. The second thing that should be said is the impossibility of assessing Gilson's legacy fairly at the present time. He did not leave us silver or gold, that can be exactly counted; he gave us what he had: a living legacy, in the students he trained, in an Institute in Toronto, and in a wealth of new ideas and perspectives. What is living can die, but it can also grow, and we cannot foresee in 1979 what the legacy will be, say, twenty-five or fifty years from now.

After these preliminary remarks I should like, rather arbitrarily, to choose three areas in which Gilson's living legacy can be found: his pupils, the Institute of Mediaeval Studies, and his ideas as expressed in his many lectures and writings.

Gilson left a large progeny of pupils both in Europe and North America. These include scholars who have made significant contributions in many fields, reflecting their master's wide range of interest. A number of these pupils are present at this symposium. One sometimes hears the expression "Gilsonian school," generally from critics of the master, but the phrase corresponds to no reality. Never was a philosopher less likely to produce a school of followers than Gilson. A school forms around a man who creates a new philosophy, like Aristotle, Descartes or Kant. Gilson made no pretension to have discovered his own philosophy. In philosophy he always preferred to be right than original. "Science is revolutionary," he said, "I am deeply convinced that philosophy is not."[1] He was unabashedly a Thomist, taking his philosophical principles from Thomas Aquinas. As for his pupils, he did not ask or demand agreement with his own ideas. He respected their freedom to come to their own conclusions. He taught them his own, but did not force them on others. In this regard, his advice to the Institute in Toronto is significant. When a professor retires or dies, he said, do not try to replace him. Find another good scholar and leave him free to develop his ideas as he wishes and as he can.

What he did demand of his students was strict adherence to scholarly methods and principles in interpreting a philosophical text. More than anything else, his students are united in the use of these principles. The first of these is fidelity to the text! The text of a philosopher (or anyone else) must be studied for itself and seen in the perspective of its author, not from someone else's viewpoint. Duns Scotus should not be interpreted through Thomas Aquinas, nor Aquinas through his commentators Cajetan and John of St. Thomas. Muslim philosophers should be read from a Muslim, not from a Christian perspective—a point Gilson forcefully made in his address to the Sixth International Congress of Philosophy in 1926.[2] To reject this principle was to put the pupil outside the pale of Gilson's discipleship. I vividly recall a seminar in which he criticized a student for his handling of a text of Boethius. The student had the audacity to reply, "But Professor Gilson, I do not accept your method." We sat in stunned silence, until Gilson broke it saying: "Then there is no point in proceeding," and gathering up his papers he left the room.

Nothing gave Gilson more pleasure than to read a newly edited text. This he did with uncanny perception into the author's basic principles and sources. He had an extraordinary ability to enter sympathetically into the author's thought and to express it clearly and profoundly. It did not matter whether the writer was Augustine, Aquinas, Bonaventure, Bernard, Dante, Duns Scotus or Descartes. He could immerse himself for a while in the mentality of the man, even though he profoundly disagreed with him. One can read the six hundred masterful pages of his book on Duns Scotus without realizing that Gilson himself once said that he could not live in the mental universe of Scotus. This love of texts, and the ability to read them, was one of the most important legacies Gilson passed on to his students.

The second legacy of Gilson I should like to discuss is the Institute of Mediaeval Studies he founded in Toronto. Others were instrumental in this foundation, but his was the guiding spirit. It was, and still is, his Institute. Emerson wrote that an institution is "the lengthened shadow of one man,"[3] and this is certainly true of the Toronto Institute. Gilson tried in vain to set up an institute devoted to medieval studies in Paris, but when this plan came to nothing, he accepted the invitation of the Basilians in Toronto to locate the institute there. Gilson conceived the Institute as a center of specialized, interdisciplinary research and teaching in medieval culture. Its aim and purpose is "to contribute, by an intensive study of the original sources and documents, to a full and accurate understanding of medieval culture in its whole scope and its many aspects and phases, and to interpret the life and thought of the Middle Ages to the modern world."[4] As a trained historian of philosophy, Gilson was concerned above all with the philosophical ideas of the Middle Ages, and particularly with those of Thomas Aquinas, but he realized that they could not be understood apart from their historical and cultural setting. The program of the Institute was therefore broadened to include theology, history, paleography, law, literature both Latin and vernacular, liturgy, art and archeology.

When the Institute was founded fifty years ago, it was the only center of medieval studies in the world. It proved so successful that many other universities in the United States and Canada began their own interdisciplinary programs of medieval studies. The most ambitious of these is in the University of Toronto, where a Centre for Medieval Studies was opened in 1964. Some forty or fifty professors not in the Pontifical Institute were teaching subjects in the medieval field, and these were brought together, along with the Institute professors, into a new center for medieval studies. At present there are about 140 graduate students in the Toronto Centre for Medieval Studies—one of the largest groups of graduate students in the University. From the start, the Pontifical Institute collaborated with the new university center and now its Licentiate Programme has been amalgamated with the larger university center as a stream leading to the Ph.D.

Though Gilson created the Toronto Institute as an historical research and teaching center, his interest in doing so was not purely historical. He did not want to go back to the Middle Ages as to a golden era. He said that he would not have wanted to live in the Middle Ages. But he was convinced that the Christian Middle Ages had something of value to offer to the modern world, and he lectured and wrote prodigiously to make that message heard.

Let me give but one example: the paper he delivered at the Harvard Tercentenary in 1937 on "Medieval Universalism and its Present Value."[5] The aim of this address, he said, "is to describe a certain aspect of medieval thought and medieval culture that can be rightly considered so typical of that period, and whose lasting value is so high that everything should be done in order to revive it under some form suitable to our own times." "I am alluding," Gilson continued, "to the deeply-rooted medieval conviction that though the various expressions of truth unavoidably bear the mark of their local origins, truth itself, both in the speculative and in the practical order, is not true for a certain civilization, nor for a certain nation, but belongs to mankind as a whole. In short, truth is universal in its own right."

Gilson had no illusion that most modern philosophers would agree with this. Quite the contrary; most of them are of the opinion that truth is always relative to a particular culture, language or epoch. But in Gilson's view this fails to do justice to human reason. Each of us has a mind that is right or true because it conforms to reality. There are many minds, but they can agree because the reality they feed upon is the same for all. The medieval philosophers, for all their differences, were united in their conviction that the human mind can know reality and rise to a knowledge of universal truths—truths that hold for all times and for all peoples. These philosophers were rationalists, Gilson said, in that they defended the dignity and power of human reason. They were also realists in their conviction that there is an objective order of reality that reason discovers and does not make. These are the foundations of medieval universalism: that truth, morality, and social justice are necessary and universal in their own right. This lesson, still to be learned from the Middle Ages, Gilson concluded, contains the basis of intellectual and social liberty. It will save us from the worst kind of slavery to which mankind is now being submitted by totalitarian states: slavery of the mind.

Gilson came to appreciate the value of medieval philosophy while a doctoral candidate at the Sorbonne. Up until then he had not read a line of Thomas Aquinas or any of the other great medieval thinkers. He had been schooled in Descartes and other modern philosophers. When his director suggested that he inquire into the scholastic background of Descartes, he became acquainted for the first time with Aquinas and other scholastic theologians. Much to his surprise he discovered that Descartes had taken over a large number of their notions and conclusions, and, even more disturbing, he found that these were better understood and defended by the scholastics than by Descartes. He describes this experience in vivid terms in his intellectual autobiography *The Philosopher and Theology*: "From scholasticism to Cartesianism the loss in metaphysical substance seemed to me frightening."[6] Writing forty-five years after the event, he recalls the feeling of fear he experienced on the day when, after holding back his pen for a long time, he finally wrote this simple sentence: "On all these points the thought of Descartes, in comparison with the sources from which it derives, marks much less a gain than a loss."[7]

This was a decisive moment—perhaps the turning point—in Gilson's intellectual life. From then on he became an avid reader of the great medieval thinkers, especially Thomas Aquinas. Gilson, the historian of medieval philosophy, was born. As his books on Aquinas, Bonaventure, the *Spirit of Mediaeval Philosophy* appeared, the reality and value of medieval philosophy became evident to all who had eyes to see. No longer could it be said with the French historian Octave Hamelin, that Descartes "is in succession with the ancients, almost as if—with the exception of a few naturalists—there had been nothing but a blank between."[8] Gilson had decisively disproven the generally accepted notion that nothing of philosophical value was discovered between the Greeks and the moderns. Other historians of medieval philosophy had a part in this, but it is due to Gilson more than to anyone else that today the Middle Ages is recognized as a vital epoch in the history of philosophy and that medieval philosophy is accepted as an indispensable subject in our universities.

As Gilson read the medieval authors, a second conviction formed in his mind. Not only did they philosophize more wisely than the modern philosophers he was studying: their excellence in philosophy was owing to the fact that they philosophized as Christians, under the influence of the light of faith. Unlike Descartes, no one of them tried to separate his philosophy from his Christian faith, but welcomed the Christian revelation as an aid to philosophy. In his Gifford Lectures on *The Spirit of Mediaeval Philosophy* he calls this concrete historical situation Christian philosophy. This he describes as "every philosophy which, although keeping the two orders (of reason and faith) formally distinct, nevertheless considers the Christian revelation as an indispensable auxiliary to reason."[9]

It is important to notice that Gilson did not consider this to be the abstract definition of a simple essence (as you might define the essence of man as 'rational animal'), but rather as the description of a concrete historical reality. Failure to appreciate this has led to misunderstanding about Gilson's notion of Christian philosophy. He readily agreed that philosophy in itself, in its formal essence, cannot be Christian. As such, philosophy is a work of human reason; it is therefore purely rational. Nothing of faith or the supernatural can be a constitutive element in its texture.[10] From this point of view he would agree with Heid-

egger that the notion of Christian philosophy is a contradiction in terms, like the notion of a square circle.[11] What
Gilson meant by Christian philosophy is something quite
different. As a philosophy, it is purely rational, held by the
light of reason alone, though the higher light of faith has
enabled the philosopher's reason to see the truths it contains. Christian philosophy, as a consequence, is a "body
of rational truths, discovered, explored or simply safe-
guarded, thanks to the help that reason receives from
revelation."[12] As an eminent example Gilson offered the
philosophy of St. Thomas. Thomist philosophy, he remarked in the Preface to the last (6th) edition of *Le
Thomisme*, is "strictly rational,"[13] and yet it was achieved
through the indispensable aid of revelation.

Gilson almost despaired of making himself understood
on this point. He once lamented that he had ever used the
expression "Christian philosophy," for it had led to so
much misunderstanding and confusion. But he never
abandoned the term. For him, it expresses an historical
reality easily identifiable by anyone who reads the medieval documents.

Fernand Van Steenberghen, among others, accused him
of establishing a kind of hybrid, a "sort of speculation
intermediary between philosophy as such and theology."[14] Gilson replied that he never dreamed of inventing this monster. "Quite to the contrary," he continued,
"those who speak of 'Christian philosophy' and the
Encyclical *Aeterni Patris* in the first place, maintain at the
same time as an unshakable principle that philosophy and
theology are two sciences formally distinct by their principles and by their objects. There is, therefore, nothing, nor
is it proposed to introduce anything, between the one and
the other." Nature does not cease to be nature when it is
elevated to the state of grace. Similarly, philosophy does
not cease to be philosophy when it is placed in the new

situation of being guided and regulated by Christian faith. "Philosophy is not more a philosophy when it is pagan than when it is Christian," Gilson wrote; "it is then only an obscured philosophy. Philosophy is not less a philosophy when it is Christian than when it is pagan, nor is it more so; but it is better."[15]

Gilson formulated his views on Christian philosophy as early as his Gifford Lectures of 1931-32, published as *The Spirit of Mediaeval Philosophy*. The first two lectures concern the problem and concept of Christian philosophy. He had written the first volume of these lectures, he tells us, without thinking of the notion of Christian philosophy. "It was then that the idea struck me," he writes, "and as it seemed to me to give a unity to the philosophy which I was in the act of describing, I wrote the first two chapters on that notion."[16] The rest of the story, he warns his reader, is hardly believable. He had completely forgotten the encyclical *Aeterni Patris*, and it was only afterwards, when he was looking through documents on the notion of Christian philosophy, that he came across it and found in it the very idea he was trying to justify in the twenty Gifford Lectures.

Gilson tells of these events leading up to the reading of *Aeterni Patris* in his *Christianity and Philosophy*, which appeared in French about five years after the Gifford Lectures. What did he mean by saying that he had completely forgotten the encyclical when he was writing these lectures? That he had read it but had forgotten its contents, or that he had forgotten that there was such an encyclical and had not read it? Many years later, in his *The Philosopher and Theology*, he cleared up this ambiguity. He confesses, to his confusion, that in fact he had not read the encyclical before preparing the Gifford Lectures.[17] If Gilson's memory was not at fault (and I know of no evidence that it was), he came to his notion of Christian philosophy independently of *Aeterni Patris*.

Gilson was struck by the fact that Leo XIII did not give a definition of Christian philosophy in his encyclical but rather a description of it as a certain way of philosophizing. Neither does he attempt to codify Christian philosophy as a particular body of doctrines, not even those of Thomas Aquinas. He simply describes it as the best way to philosophize because it unites the study of philosophy with docility to the teachings of divine revelation. Far from enslaving reason, this "bond of friendship" between reason and faith is said to be a source of many benefits to both. Leo XIII, moreover, appeals to history to furnish examples of this way of philosophizing: the Church Fathers and especially Augustine, the medieval doctors, particularly Bonaventure and Aquinas. After reading *Aeterni Patris* Gilson realized that he had spent much time and research to find out something he could have learned with a little attention to the teaching of the Church. But then, he adds, philosophers of his day did not often read papal encyclicals.[18]

After this experience we can appreciate Gilson's unbounded admiration for Leo XIII. To him, the Pope was the "greatest Christian philosopher of the nineteenth century and one of the greatest of all time."[19] He edited *Aeterni Patris* with eight other encyclicals of Leo XIII in the Image Book *The Church Speaks to the Modern World. The Social Teachings of Leo XIII.*[20] Following the suggestion of Leo himself, Gilson placed *Aeterni Patris* first among these encyclicals because it gives the doctrinal foundation for all the social documents that follow.

Gilson's autobiographical *The Philosopher and Theology* not only clarifies his relation to *Aeterni Patris*; it also throws precious light on the development of his understanding of Thomistic philosophy. He first studied St. Thomas, he explains, as though he were a philosopher, and indeed he felt justified in doing so because he found a good deal of philosophizing in his works. But as he examined St. Thomas' notion of theology more closely, he realized that for St. Thomas theology is a science containing not only truths held on faith or deduced from them, but also notions and truths accessible to pure human reason. In St. Thomas' view, everything in the *Summa Theologiae* is theological, even those philosophical doctrines developed in the context of theology and used for theological purposes. So Gilson was led to the unexpected conclusion that what he had called Thomistic philosophy was in fact a part of Thomistic theology—the part that St. Thomas considered to be demonstrable by reason.

What then becomes of Thomistic philosophy? It does not cease to exist. St. Thomas was indeed a philosopher (a *philosophans*, to use the medieval term), and it is possible to extract the elements of a philosophy from his theology. This is what Gilson has done in his *Le Thomisme. Introduction à la Philosophie de Saint Thomas d'Aquin*; also in his *Elements of Christian Philosophy*.[21] This philosophy is rational in that it appeals to reason, not to faith, for its truth; it is also Christian because it is the handmaid of theology and belongs to its household.

The legacy of Gilson's writings is so prodigious and varied in theme and style that it defies neat classification. Among his books in philosophy, however, it is possible to distinguish three types. First, there are the strictly historical books, like those on Descartes, Bonaventure, Thomas Aquinas, Duns Scotus, and the histories of philosophy. Here, Gilson the philosopher is surely present, but his purpose is not to set forth his own views but those of others.

The second group of books looks like histories of philosophy, but they are not. They include some of Gilson's most influential works: *The Unity of Philosophical Experience* and *Being and Some Philosophers*. In the preface to the latter, Gilson says: "...this is not a book in the history of philosophy; it is a philosophical book, and a dogmatically philosophical one at that....every line of this book is philosophic, if not in form, at least in its purpose."[22] There is so much about other philosophers in the book that its philosophical character can easily be missed, and indeed one reviewer did criticize it for historical lapses, forgetting that Gilson had warned of its "historical arbitrariness."[23] Time and again *The Unity of Philosophical Experience* has been criticized as though it were a history of philosophy. It has been said, for example, that Ockham has been unfairly treated in it, as though Gilson made any pretension here to give an historical account of Ockhamism![24] In fact, though *The Unity of Philosophical Experience* is filled with the history of philosophical ideas, its whole purpose is philosophical and not historical.

To what philosophical genre do these books belong? They are examples of what Gilson calls philosophical reflection on the history of philosophy. Every philosopher philosophizes from the data most accessible and best known to him, as Aristotle philosophized from biological data and Descartes from mathematics. Most ready to Gilson's hand was the history of philosophy, and he used it brilliantly to gain insights of philosophical value. A striking example is the concluding chapter of *The Unity of Philosophical Experience*, which is rich in lessons for the philosopher drawn from the experience of reading the history of philosophy.

Gilson describes this method of philosophizing in a paper published in 1953 entitled "Expérience et Métaphysique."[25] It is, he says, a sort of experimentation on philosophical data furnished by history. He hastens to add that this will never replace strict philosophical method, but he defends it as a secondary and auxiliary method of philosophizing.

The third group of books in philosophy left by Gilson is so clearly the expression of his own views that they would never be confused with the history of philosophy. I refer to his three books on the philosophy of art: *Painting and Reality*, *The Arts of the Beautiful*, and *Forms and Substances in the Arts*; also to his book on the philosophy of language (*Linguistique et Philosophie*) and his book on finality in nature and evolution (*D'Aristote à Darwin et Retour*). The latter book he calls a study in the philosophy of life or "biophilosophie." In all these books Gilson the philosopher is clearly at work, though never without an eye on the history of ideas.

He wrote the books on art with an unusual sense of urgency and compulsion. Writing was a passion with him; he speaks of himself when he describes "the need to write, which is so intense for some people that its frustration is painful."[26] On finishing the third book on art (*Forms and Substances in the Arts*) he breathed a sigh of relief. He had finally expressed, he said, all he had in him on the subject. He was a great lover and connoisseur of painting, poetry and music; indeed he once told me he thought he had listened to music more in his life than he had read philosophy. It was a joy for him to philosophize on his beloved subject of the arts. As early as 1916 he published an article entitled "Art et Métaphysique."[27] When he took up the philosophy of art again, forty years later, he had behind him a lifetime of reflection on the fine arts and a deepened appreciation of St. Thomas' metaphysics of existence.

The theme running through all his writings on the philosophy of art is that art belongs to the order of making or "facticity," not to the order of knowledge. The fine arts, he insists, aim at the production of beautiful things; they are not essentially a kind of knowledge or an intuition—not even a creative intuition, as his friend Jacques Maritain would have it. For once Gilson was critical of the scholastics, who, like Aristotle, defined art as the correct idea to follow in matters of production: *recta ratio factibilium*. Gilson recognized that intelligence is at play in the arts, but he resisted all attempts to place the whole of art on the side of the mind.[28]

These philosophical works of Gilson are examples of what he called living Thomism, i.e. a creative use of Thomistic principles in facing contemporary philosophical issues. He points out that modern Thomists are confronted with problems unknown to St. Thomas, for which no answers can be found ready-made in his writings. As a consequence Thomism is bound to create if it is still to live. Gilson considered Jacques Maritain an eminent example of a living Thomist. He wrote: "In the fields of the philosophy of nature, of political economy and of the so-called 'human sciences,' the example of Jacques Maritain clearly shows how it is still possible today to renovate ancient concepts and to open new fields of investigation."[29] Gilson himself was busy at this throughout his life, and his own living Thomism is one of his most precious legacies.

Gilson not only gave us a living Thomism; he also showed us how to philosophize as a Christian—in Leo XIII's words, how to unite the study of philosophy with docility to the teachings of faith. Gilson was many things: a man of letters, a humanist, an historian of philosophy and a philosopher, but he was above all a man of faith. He loved philosophy, but he loved his faith more, and he never tired in putting his intelligence in the service of faith.

"Intelligence in the Service of Christ the King": how well this title of one of his essays sums up the man Gilson![30] Christ was to him, as he was to St. John and the great doctors of the Church, the Word of God, who enlightens everyone who comes into the world. When Gilson was dying in the hospital, the chaplain saw his name on the list of patients, and he wondered if this could

be the Gilson he admired so much. Entering his room, he
realized that it was, and bending down he said to Gilson:
"If it were permitted, I would call you my master." Gilson
looked up and quoted our Lord's words: *One is your master,
Christ* (Matt. 23, 10).

As for intelligence, how richly he was endowed with it!
And how he loved the mind! He liked to quote St. Augustine: "Love intelligence and love it very dearly" (*intellectum
valde ama*).[31] He prized all the works of the mind: science,
philosophy, theology, art, music, poetry. Nothing intellectual was alien to him. If he set such high standards of
excellence for himself and his pupils, it was because of his
great reverence for the mind and truth. And why did he
love the mind? Because it is the crown of creation. God
made man in his own image and likeness, and, as St.
Augustine assures us, this image is found in the mind: *in
mente.*

Gilson was repelled by the Lutheran notion that the fall
of man totally corrupted human nature, including man's
mind. The Catholic Church, he points out, teaches the
contrary. It professes before everything the restoration of
wounded nature by the grace of Jesus Christ; and if there is
a restoration of nature, there must be a nature, and of what
value, since it is the work of God, who both created it and
recreated it by the blood of Christ.[32]

Equally abhorrent to Gilson was the idea that nature and
intelligence should be separated from Christ. Looking back
on his Sorbonne days, he recalls with astonishment his
Catholic professors of philosophy whose Catholicism had
not the slightest influence on their teaching. Indeed, he
did not know until later that some of them were
Catholics.[33] To Gilson, these men missed the point that the
mind must be restored, healed and sanctified by the grace
of Christ; only then will it be at its finest and produce its
best works. The great Christian thinkers were witnesses to

this: St. Augustine, St. Bonaventure, St. Thomas Aquinas, Pascal, Malebranche. Gilson loved these men; he read and reread them, emulated them, for they recognized the primacy of the word of God and of theology. They were indeed Christian theologians and philosophers. They united their study of philosophy and their faith, and they knew how to put their intelligence in the service of Christ. "To seize truth here below by the intelligence," Gilson wrote, "be it in an obscure and partial manner, while waiting to see it in its complete splendor—such is man's destiny according to Christianity."[34] In his own way, and in a modern setting, Gilson has shown us how to fulfill this destiny.

1. E. Gilson, *D'Aristote à Darwin et Retour* (Paris: J. Vrin, 1971), p. 10.

2. "Le rôle de la philosophie dans l'histoire de la civilisation," *Proceedings of the Sixth International Congress of Philosophy*, Harvard, 1926 (New York and London, 1927), pp. 529-535.

3. R.W. Emerson, essay on Self-Reliance.

4. G.B. Flahiff, "The Pontifical Institute of Mediaeval Studies in Toronto," *Speculum*, 24 (1949): 252.

5. Published in *Independence, Convergence and Borrowing in Institutions, Thought and Art* (Cambridge, Mass.: Harvard Univ. Press, 1937).

6. *The Philosopher and Theology*, trans. C. Gilson (New York: Random House, 1962), p. 88.

7. Ibid., pp. 88-89.

8. See E. Gilson, *The Spirit of Mediaeval Philosophy*, trans. A.H.C. Downes (New York: Scribner's, 1940), p. 13.

9. Ibid., p. 37.

10. Ibid.

11. See M. Heidegger, *An Introduction to Metaphysics*, trans. R. Manheim (New York: Doubleday, 1961), p. 6.

12. *The Spirit of Mediaeval Philosophy*, p. 35.

13. *Le Thomisme. Introduction à la Philosophie de Saint Thomas d'Aquin* (Paris: J. Vrin, 1965), p. 7. The fifth edition of this work was translated by L.K. Shook with the title *The Christian Philosophy of St. Thomas Aquinas* (New York: Random House, 1956).

14. *Christianity and Philosophy*, trans. R. MacDonald (New York: Sheed & Ward, 1939), p. 95.

15. Ibid., p. 87.

16. Ibid., p. 93.

17. *The Philosopher and Theology*, p. 180.

18. Ibid. See *Christianity and Philosophy*, p. 94.

19. *The Philosopher and Theology*, p. 218.

20. (New York: Doubleday, 1954).

21. (New York: Doubleday, 1960).

22. *Being and Some Philosophers*, 2nd ed. (Toronto: Pontifical Institute of Mediaeval Studies, 1952), pp. ix-x.

23. Ibid., p. x. See the review by John Wild in *Speculum*, 24 (1949): 573-578.

24. See, for example, P. Boehner, "The Notitia Intuitiva of Non-Existents according to William Ockham," *Traditio*, 1 (1943): 223-275; S. Day, *Intuitive Cognition: A Key to the Significance of the Later Scholastics* (St. Bonaventure: Franciscan Institute, 1947).

25. *Actes du XIe Congrès International de Philosophie*, 1953, vol. IV (Amsterdam and Louvain, 1953), pp. 5-10.

26. *The Arts of the Beautiful* (New York: Scribner's, 1965), p. 80.

27. *Revue de Métaphysique et de Morale*, 23 (1916): 243-267.

28. *The Arts of the Beautiful*, pp. 81-82. See J. Maritain, *Creative Intuition in Art and Poetry* (New York: Pantheon Books, 1953); *Art and Scholasticism*, trans J.F. Scanlan (London: Sheed & Ward, 1933), p. 13.

29. E. Gilson, *The Spirit of Thomism* (New York: P.J. Kenedy & Sons, 1964), p. 100.

30. *A Gilson Reader*, ed. A.C. Pegis (New York: Doubleday, 1957). The essay is chapter 5 of *Christianity and Philosophy*.

31. "Intelligence in the Service of Christ the King," *A Gilson Reader*, p. 33.

32. Ibid., p. 37.

33. *The Philosopher and Theology*, p. 35.

34. "Intelligence in the Service of Christ the King," *A Gilson Reader*, p. 32.

The Legacy of Jacques Maritain, Christian Philosopher

Donald A. Gallagher

De Rance Foundation, Milwaukee, Wisconsin

In the minds and hearts of those who knew or were deeply influenced by him from the 1930s on, including a number of us participants in this *Aeterni Patris* Symposium, the figure of Jacques Maritain remains vivid. A figure everlastingly young. He had just attained fifty years of age, and was in the prime of his intellectual life when he first visited North America. He had just published his master work, *The Degrees of Knowledge*,[1] and was soon to publish *Integral Humanism*.[2] Still in the picture we formed of him, in those days from the news and the articles reaching us a bit belatedly from Europe, Maritain stood forth as the ardent convert, the militant Thomist who held up St. Thomas as the apostle for our time,[3] the young Christian philosopher hailed by Léon Bloy as the *lamentateur*, which I render freely as "a lamenting or anguished prophetic voice."

For forty years thereafter the extraordinary career of our Christian philosopher unfolded. And so to those of a later generation he stands forth as an old sage, a philosopher who dedicated his mind to a lifetime of service to Christ, the scholar who received from the hands of Pope Paul VI at the end of Vatican II in December 1965, when he was already eighty-three years old, the message to the intellectuals of the world. He stands forth as the old Christian layman, the *vieux paysan*, who fearlessly speaks out in a controversial book about the ills, but also the accomplishments, of our time. And he stands forth as our "little brother Jacques" of the Little Brothers of Jesus.

Personally, I treasure the memory of my last visit with him at Toulouse in January, 1973. He died in April, a few months later. My colleague, the President of the De Rance Foundation, and I had the privilege of a private audience with Pope Paul who spoke movingly of Maritain and uttered the words, "*è un santo*." I brought a message from His Holiness to Jacques, whose small room was adorned with pictures and photographs only of Raïssa, both as young and in her later age, and of the Pope. It was extraordinary to see this humble figure just over ninety with the young Little Brothers who looked upon him with an indefinable combination of reverence and of comradeship. They employed the "thee-thou", the *tutoyer*, in addressing one another, which as I understood was somewhat unusual for Maritain, who was familiar in many of his relationships, but did not always go that far, even with people he knew well.

This venerable personage ready for eternity, as he told me, still had something of him, of the young man with the gentle face, a heavy shock of blond hair, a light beard, and a slightly stooped carriage, of whom Raïssa speaks, and as she describes him in *Les grandes amitiés*.[4]

What now of the legacy of Maritain? Legacy with all its specific meanings has overtones for us in the realm of culture. It may be exerting a dynamic influence or be inert. Much depends upon what we bring to it, as well as upon what we are receiving. If by some unthinkable catastrophe Shakespeare were no longer played or even read, his legacy might still be there on the shelf, but without communicativeness. The legacy of Maritain may be envisaged from the aspects of gift, bequest, and commission.

His legacy as his gift to us I take to mean his life and his endeavors in a number of domains. I extend it to include his gift of himself, his wisdom, his love, to those who are to come after him. Much as St. Thomas is a guide and an example for us so many years after his death, so Maritain is destined, I believe, to be one, particularly for laymen and laywomen in the generations to come.

The legacy as bequest I take to mean the vast and varied philosophical corpus he has bequeathed to us. We all know how immense his labors, his output were in this respect. Idella and I calculated in our bibliography, *The Achievement of Jacques and Raïssa Maritain,*[5] (and I might add here how delighted Jacques was with the fact that we so entitled it with the two names together), that he had published at that time several hundred articles, actually over four hundred. Although many were the same one in different languages, still each was an event in its own time and place. There were about seventy-five books, some of them essays printed in book form, and others which overlapped in content with other books; still the number is large. Please pardon this extended reference to his considerable output. What a sad word that is, smacking of quantity, rather than quality, conjuring up an image of one banging away at a typewriter to keep a production schedule, rather than meditating on being, and knowing and loving. But the reference is made to convey an idea of his unflagging labors over so long a lifetime. Often he would write in letters (I have several myself)—in which the expression occurs—of how he was overwhelmed with work, *je suis accablé par les travaux.*

In 1933 when he first came among us on this continent, he had written some twenty books. By the 1970s, about forty years later, some sixty more.

In re-reading the Maritain corpus, which I tried to do afresh as though reading him for the first time, the impact of what is meant by Christian philosophy—and what he meant by it—struck me with new force. All of us are familiar undoubtedly with the role of Christian philosophy in the thought of Maritain. It bears pondering again in our present situation as we commemorate *Aeterni Patris* and as we look to the future. For this purpose I shall offer some thoughts taken from a selection of his works and present Maritain himself as our Christian philosopher. This presentation will prepare the way for a brief consideration of Maritain's legacy to us in the third sense I mentioned, a commission, that is, a kind of charge he places upon us to elaborate a Thomistic philosophy which is truly autonomous. The autonomy of philosophy, as he tells us in *The Peasant of the Garonne*,[6] and as he has said expressly in a number of other places, has never really been accomplished. He says, for example, in *Existence and the Existent*[7] and equivalently in *Science and Wisdom*,[8] that St. Thomas had set forth the autonomy in principle, but that it was never truly established in fact. This is what he calls upon us to do in a new age of culture to come.

The topics Maritain writes about are, as we know, extremely varied. In all cases, except for a few extremely technical and specialized topics, the influence, the impact, the light of Christian thought and revelation are evidently discernible. There are topics which are properly philosophical; there are others which may properly be treated by both the theologian and the philosopher, according to their respective lights; there are again those which are undoubtedly theological or pertain even to the religious and spiritual life. For example, in *On the Grace and Humanity of Jesus*,[9] he treats of the life of Jesus from the Virgin Birth to the Passion and the Death on the Cross, and refers explicitly to the fact that he is treating theological topics, yet insists that he is looking at them from the perspective of a philosopher, trying to get some meaning which will help in his understanding of life.

I should like to point out here that as I proceed to a rapid survey of the illustrations—of key illustrations—of such topics from his writings, I may touch upon questions which are arguable or debatable among Thomists. Some may disagree with a particular position of his in metaphysics, or with his particular view of moral philosophy (that of course is a very celebrated topic and one that still should be gone into more thoroughly). Others may argue that he is treating this or that topic theologically, and perhaps in an illegitimate manner. Yet all the while Maritain himself insists that he is remaining on the philosophical plane. My task as I view it here is not to defend any of these positions but rather to point out Maritain, the Christian philosopher, as he characteristically works, and to show how the results and the method he employs provide a model for us. And if on the whole we accept what he is offering to us, we are accepting his legacy. We may then make this legacy our own by our own philosophical effort of personal reflection and appropriation of truth as we reason and argue it out by ourselves.

The notion of Christian philosophy matured in the mind of Maritain over a period of years. It was the controversies on the subject in the 1930s that stimulated him to write his essay "On Christian Philosophy."[10] If I am not mistaken, it was in 1933 that he wrote it, the very year that he first came to Canada and the United States. This is not the occasion to reopen the question, whether there is or can be such a thing. What matters here is to see this conception as the directive idea which explains his own philosophizing and what it led to. The term itself "Christian philosophy" he says on more than one occasion scarcely enchants him. It smacks of a pious confraternity. Yet, he said, it was good enough for Leo XIII, and if it is explained properly we can and should retain it. In one of his later works, he uses a word like "ontosophy" and he opposes philosophy and ideosophy.[11] And this leads to another theme in Maritain which I digress upon just for a moment here—his sensitivity to language, vocabulary, terminology. He feels that even the noblest terms often become routine, and although he does not mean to coin new terms for the sake of novelty, or having something distinctive for his own work, nevertheless he feels at times that to shock people, as it were, back to thinking about the reality to which the term points, it may be necessary to coin a new term.

Once more, what matters in all of this, is that we are not simply engaged in a theoretical exposition of the nature and the status of Christian philosophy, though that is very important to understand rightly. We should realize that the philosopher should join his philosophic labors and his life of prayer in a living, organic unity, all the while safeguarding the purity and the rigor of philosophy. This is the path Maritain charted for himself for the years to come.

In the preface to *The Degrees of Knowledge*, already referred to, published in 1932, Maritain after carefully explaining the methodology he is pursuing in reviewing the vast and varied expanses of human knowing, not in the manner of a didactic treatise, but in the manner of exploring and meditating upon the significance of these knowledges, makes the comment that when a philosopher adopts as the object of his study something which impinges upon the existential conditions of the human being, he can proceed scientifically only if he respects the integrity of his object and consequently the integrity of those realities of the supernatural order which are implied in it.[12] Thus does he answer the reproach of those who say he is not remaining on the plane of pure philosophy.

This vision of Christian philosophy we now are able to

enjoy thanks to Maritain whose manner of philosophizing is a decisive moment in the history of western culture. His habit of setting topics, questions, in their cultural context is important for Maritain. He seems to be concerned with two aspects: one, to bring out in the most exact way what the theoretical bearing of a question is, and the other, to show us where it is situated in culture. So, he feels that in developing this conception of Christian philosophy we have arrived at a *prise de conscience* which is a true historic gain. Yet, at the same time, as mentioned already, he feels that the fullness of this Christian philosophy and all of the various areas and domains of philosophy have yet to be worked out. He points out, for example, that the style of the medieval age of culture is that of the differentiation and of the acme of theology, while that of the modern age of culture is that of the birth and development of philosophy. However, it has been philosophy in schism, as he puts it. So therefore what is needed is an age in which an authentically Christian philosophy differentiates itself and takes on its proper dimensions.

We may note here in passing his comment, which has to be understood properly, that St. Thomas was not a cultural success in his own medieval intellectual world; he really came into his own centuries later, and then perhaps only for a short period. Supposing that we shall have another renewal of Thomistic studies, we may ask in turn what will the legacy of Maritain be in this respect? Will it be like that of Aquinas? Will he come into his own after a lapse of time? Whether the Maritain revival occurs in the 1990s or the 2090s, we may be confident it will emerge into the light of day at the providential moment when most needed. But there are those of us who see it occurring here and there already, in Italy above all, in Venezuela and even, here and there, at home.

Just as in philosophy there is still so much to do, so,

according to Maritain, in social and political life and in the economic field we are in a primitive stage. As appears throughout the pages of *True Humanism*, in terms of an effective socio-temporal realization of the gospel message we are still prehistoric. While reading a number of his works on social thought such as *True Humanism*,[13] *The Twilight of Civilization*,[14] *Christianity and Democracy*,[15] *The Rights of Man and the Natural Law*,[16] so often I was hearing at the same time Pope John Paul II because as I was reading these books, the Pope was about to visit the United States and his messages and words were being repeated on television and printed in the papers.

The Twilight of Civilization (1939) is a tract for the times. It sums up the theme of *True Humanism*: the conflict between theocentric and anthropocentric humanism, except that here he confronts the tragedy threatening western civilization which was soon to break out in the war. And he writes here with words of fire, like a prophet, as a Christian philosopher, voicing indignation at the appalling consequences of humanism without God, which endeavors to organize the human race into a body the supreme destiny of which is to gain domination over the earth, with no regard for anything else.

It is not possible to treat and even refer to in survey fashion all the texts relevant to our thesis: Maritain the Christian philosopher and the legacy he leaves us. But it would be easy to arrange passages from many works in which he refers to the key role of Christianity itself and of the task confronting Christian philosophy in the future.

Some of the most significant passages occur in the works of his later, or even last, period by which I mean those after 1958 or after he was seventy-five years of age. One should dwell upon the lengthy and magisterial section, "The Impact of Christianity on Moral Philosophy," in his book entitled *Moral Philosophy*.[17] One should also dwell upon what he says about the pre-conscious of the spirit and the advent of the self in western thought under the impact of the Christian influence, in *Creative Intuition in Art and Poetry*,[18] and upon what he says about the consciousness of Jesus in *On the Grace and Humanity of Jesus*.[19] This last book, by the way, originated as did some of the short works of his last years in what he called "research seminars," given originally to the Little Brothers of Jesus who have their house of studies in Toulouse near the great Dominican center where they took their courses in philosophy and theology. So he presents his thinking on a topic of this kind, the Grace and Humanity of Jesus, in the context first of all of researches, as he calls them.[20] He is exploring; he is probing; he does not intend to say anything definitive, but always insists that he is looking at these topics not as a theologian—"I am not a theologian"[21]—but only as a simple layman with years of teaching philosophy and with years of meditating and praying about these matters. That is how he puts it.

The same thing is said in *The Church of Christ* on the mystery of the Church, on the Church as person.[22] Above all, in a posthumous work, *Approches sans entraves*,[23] in one essay after the other he takes up topics, for example, on the priesthood, even on the sacred eucharist, subtle metaphysical questions, which are once again, he says, viewed from the perspective of philosophy. This would be a case where one might argue with him and ask whether these pages are properly speaking philosophical, or are they trespassing on another domain? Nevertheless there is undoubtedly much of philosophical value and matter for philosophical insight in his reflections on these exalted topics. The editor of *Approches sans entraves* has as his *nom de plume* Ernst R. Korn, but I understand that he really is Brother Heinz Schmitz, who is now director of studies for the Little Brothers of Jesus. In his introduction to the book, the editor in effect calls Maritain a "theo-philosopher."[24] Is this just a way of getting around this whole question of theology and philosophy, for what is he saying exactly by calling him a kind of theo-philosopher? There may be a comparison here with what Maritain says in that beautiful passage about St. Augustine in *The Degrees of Knowledge* to the effect that in one way St. Augustine is not really a theologian or a philosopher at all, he is sort of super-eminently both; he is more eminently the theologian and more virtually the philosopher.[25] Maritain is a kind of sage, especially in his later years, and he is stating it thus from the perspective of a later period of cultural differentiation. Augustine himself, of course, stands at the very fountain-head of Christian thinking and development before all the distinctions were made in theology and philosophy by later thinkers. In a way Maritain embodies all these things, which are no doubt distinct and must be distinct, yet form such a marvelous unity. As a personal reflection, I recall what Yves Simon said on this topic. It would be hard to find a philosopher who was more devotedly and avowedly a disciple of Maritain than Yves Simon and yet a truly authentic philosopher in his own right. Simon used to say somewhat humorously on the theme of distinguish in order to unite, "I think Maritain wants to do both, but he is stressing the 'unite' more. I also want to do both, but I am stressing the 'distinguish' more."

Be that as it may, this is all part of the question we face here.

I now come—yes, there is one more passage from the book that I meant not to include—I cannot refrain from commenting on this. In *God and the Permission of Evil*, another book which grew out of seminars given to the Little Brothers, this one in May 1962, Maritain remarks at the very opening of the work, that "In proportion as the conscience of men, under the very influence of Christianity, became sensible of the dignity of the human person and of the outrages which are inflicted on him by evil—the problem of evil has taken on a more tragic importance for the human conscience."[26] Out of this opening thought comes one of the most searchingly speculative and scrupulously reasoned of all his essays. Maritain himself says, "If in my philosophical work [this is in the preface to *God and the Permission of Evil*] there has perchance been some actual contribution (however imperfectly it may have been able to be presented) to the progress of thought and to the researches which announce a new age of culture [this is a phrase which is repeated in his writings from early to late] it is, indeed, so I am persuaded, the one with which this little book has to deal."[27] And this book, of course, came after the Aquinas Lecture on Evil which he gave in the 1940s.[28]

In turning our attention to the legacy in the final sense that I mentioned, the third or final sense, legacy as commission, we are provided with a number of texts from all the works of Maritain, but particularly from his later period. Above all, we are confronted with that difficult book, *The Peasant*.[29] I confess I have had to come to terms with it myself. It is harsh; it contains hard views on a number of questions which one needs to study for one's self more deeply as well as some of the philosophers and personages rejected there. We have to envisage him, however, (and this is what came to my mind in reading the book again a week or two ago), we have to look upon him as the old peasant—it is a style that he gives himself; a kind of prophet uttering warnings from the mountaintop, just as the young convert did in *Antimoderne*.[30] Although that book appeared in 1922, whereas he was baptized in 1906, it still echoes that early period of his life. Just as the young convert in *Antimoderne* inveighed against the dangers of modernity, so here too the old philosopher—the old peasant—is

inveighing against neo-modernity. He has hard sayings
about the persons and the events before Vatican Council II
(this is not often remembered); about the crisis for the
Church and civilization which was building up for generations, especially during the nineteenth century. He has
much to say, for example, about what he calls the "masked
Manicheanism" and a kind of objective Pharisaism in the
Church. And this led in many ways to the need for the
Council, the need for the positive program, but then he
heaps sarcasm upon the happenings and the individuals
since Vatican Council II: so many people, sometimes even
very mature people, not only young seminarians, but even
priests and laymen of a certain age rushing off and doing
things like adolescents. So his sarcasm is heavy in speaking of "the ruminators and the sheep of Panurge."[31] This
vivid imagery and powerful judgment deserve being
rendered with strong savage flashes of color by a Goya or
rather a Rouault.

But let us not forget there are positive things in the
book. At the very beginning his chant of joy and thanks-
giving for the gift of Vatican Council II. For one thing, the
layman, he believes, is given his status of majority at long
last, even though it will take decades before this is
achieved in reality. For our purposes here Maritain states
more bluntly and hardly than ever before that we still have
no Thomist theology fully developed, above all, no fully
autonomous and articulated Thomistic philosophy. It is as
though since Leo XIII there has been a colossal failure. Yet
he is quick to acknowledge significant contributions of a
large number of persons, including many of his own associates—teachers, colleagues and disciples. Still, in the final
reckoning he comes right out and says that so little has
been done.

Once again I think we have to see him here not speaking
in the measured tones of the philosopher, making some

kind of critical evaluation, but speaking from the mountain top, lamenting human shortcomings, including his own. He says I am not worth beans. After all he feels that in terms of the vision he has, in terms of what a comprehensive and truly majestic philosophical vision would be, almost nothing has been done.

All of this points to what I have called Maritain's commission to us; his appeal to set to work and build the Christian philosophy along the grand lines he sets forth. It is no simple task. Often he refers to modern culture with its built-in obstacles to metaphysical thinking and to spirituality. He refers to the loss of the sense of being, the sense of love, the sense of truth. Even many of the Catholic scholars, of religious-minded scholars, and persons from all fields and from various faiths and beliefs are overwhelmed by this. Often they do not even realize it. In the field of knowledge, he says we are overwhelmed by the primacy of verification over speculative truth. Everything has to be verified after the manner of the scientific methodologies. And if it cannot be, then it is something that does not exist; it is something very vague and remote.

On the other hand, however, the new age of culture which he sees as in process of formation for some time now does provide us with many gains. Here again we have this theme of the *prise de conscience*. Many historic gains, not only in knowledge but in various forms of human endeavor, have been won. These give us support. These can help in the task.

Now this task, as was brought out by so many of the speakers and discussants in our symposium, is not just for one person or one school of thought. Maritain is not calling for disciples to form a school. He would be horrified at the idea of a school of Maritainians. The very strangeness of the term shows that it is not a serious prospect. The task he puts forth is a common task: it is for all of us, even of different approaches within the Thomistic synthesis. It involves a serious return to our common master, St. Thomas. It involves a collaborative effort by scholars not only in philosophy but in various related disciplines. And above all, it involves personal philosophizing. Otherwise no true philosophy will be developed.

Now in this enterprise, what is the legacy of Maritain? He gives us his charge and makes his appeal to us. He offers his gifts, his life as a model, his works with what they contain, as aids. This is the legacy that he has left to us.

1. Jacques Maritain, *Distinguer pour unir ou Les Degrés du savoir* (Paris: Desclée de Brouwer, 1932); *The Degrees of Knowledge*, trans. Gerald B. Phelan (New York: Charles Scribner's Sons, 1959).

2. Jacques Maritain, *Humanisme intégral* (Paris: Fernand Aubier, 1936); *True Humanism*, trans. M.R. Adamson (London: Geoffrey Bles: The Centenary Press, 1938); *Integral Humanism*, trans. Joseph W. Evans (New York: Charles Scribner's Sons, 1968).

3. See Jacques Maritain, *Le Docteur angélique* (Paris: Paul Hartmann, 1929; Desclée de Brouwer, 1930); translated by J.F. Scanlan under the title *St. Thomas Aquinas Angel of the Schools* (London: Sheed and Ward, 1942). "The Apostle of our Time" is the title of Chapter III.

4. Raïssa Maritain, *Les grandes amitiés: Les aventures de la grâce* (New York: Éditions de la Maison Française, 1944); *We Have Been Friends Together*, trans. Julie Kernan (New York and Toronto: Longmans, Green and Co., 1942); *Adventures in Grace*, trans. Julie Kernan (New York and Toronto: Longmans, Green and Co., 1945). Published together as an Image Book (Garden City, New York: Doubleday, 1961). See the Image Book, p. 41.

5. Donald and Idella Gallagher, *The Achievement of Jacques and Raïssa Maritain: A Bibliography* (New York: Doubleday, 1962).

6. Jacques Maritain, *The Peasant of the Garonne*, trans. Michael Cuddihy and Elizabeth Hughes (New York: Holt, Rinehart and Winston, 1968), p. 135.

7. Jacques Maritain, *Existence and the Existent*, trans. Lewis Galantiere and Gerald B. Phelan (New York: Pantheon Books, 1948), p. 136. Published as an Image Book (Garden City, New York: Doubleday and Co., 1956) and as a Vintage Book (New York: Random House, 1966).

8. Jacques Maritain, *Science and Wisdom*, trans. Bernard Wall (London: Geoffrey Bles: The Centenary Press, 1940).

9. Jacques Maritain, *On the Grace and Humanity of Jesus*, trans. Joseph W. Evans (New York: Herder and Herder, 1969).

10. Jacques Maritain, *An Essay on Christian Philosophy*, trans. Edward H. Flannery (New York: Philosophical Library, 1955).

11. *The Peasant*, pp. 38, 98.

12. *The Degrees of Knowledge*, p. 308.

13. See note 2 above.

14. Jacques Maritain, *The Twilight of Civilization*, trans. Lionel Landry (New York: Sheed and Ward, 1943).

15. Jacques Maritain, *Christianity and Democracy*, trans. Doris C. Anson, (London: Geoffrey Bles: The Centenary Press, 1945).

16. Jacques Maritain, *The Rights of Man and the Natural Law* (London: Geoffrey Bles: The Centenary Press, 1944).

17. Jacques Maritain, *Moral Philosophy*, An Historical and Critical Survey of the Great Systems (New York: Charles Scribner's Sons, 1964).

18. Jacques Maritain, *Creative Intuition in Art and Poetry* (New York: Pantheon Books, 1953). Published as a Meridian Book (Cleveland and New York: The World Publishing Company, 1954).

19. *On the Grace and Humanity of Jesus*, pp. 48-61.

20. *On the Grace and Humanity of Jesus*, p. 7.

21. *On the Grace and Humanity of Jesus*, p. 11.

22. *On the Church of Christ*, trans. Joseph W. Evans (Notre Dame: University of Notre Dame Press, 1973), p. v.

23. Jacques Maritain, *Approches sans entraves* (Paris: Fayard, 1973).

24. *Approches sans entraves*, pp. xxii, xxiv.

25. See *The Degrees of Knowledge*, Chap. VII, Augustinian Wisdom.

26. Jacques Maritain, *God and the Permission of Evil*, trans. Joseph W. Evans (Milwaukee: The Bruce Publishing Company, 1965), p. 3.

27. *God and the Permission of Evil*, p. viii.

28. Jacques Maritain, *St. Thomas and the Problem of Evil*, The Aquinas Lecture 1942 (Milwaukee: Marquette University Press, 1942).

29. See note 9.

30. Jacques Maritain, *Antimoderne* (Paris: Éditions de la Revue des Jeunes, 1922).

31. *The Peasant*, p. 26.

Looking At
The Present

Reflections on Christian Philosophy

Ralph McInerny

The Medieval Institute, University of Notre Dame

It is not without significance for the theme of our meeting that, in a chapter entitled "Christian Philosophy" in his remarkable memoir, *The Philosopher and Theology*, Etienne Gilson discussed the encyclical *Aeterni Patris*, drawing attention to what became the traditional way of referring to it, viz. "On the Restoration in Catholic Schools of Christian Philosophy According to the Mind of the Angelic Doctor Saint Thomas Aquinas." Any discussion of the development of Gilson's thought and his altering interpretation of the writings of Saint Thomas, which can be traced through the various editions of *Le Thomisme*, must, I think, take into account the effect on him of the quarrel about the very concept of Christian Philosophy which began in 1931 and continued for some years, largely in France, and came to include many of the great figures of contemporary French philosophy, Gilson himself, Emile Bréhier who in effect began the quarrel, Jacques Maritain, Leon Brunschvicg, Van Steenberghen, Noël, Blondel and Renard, to name only the chief figures. That quarrel is discussed by Maurice Nédoncelle in his *Is There A Christian Philosophy?*[1] and André Henry in "La querelle de la philosophie chrétienne: histoire et bilan d'un débat."[2]

I do not propose to trace the outlines of that famous discussion here, nor to discuss the various works in which

Gilson returned to the question and sharpened his own position, works like *Christianisme et Philosophie* in 1949 and *Introduction à la philosophie chrétienne* in 1960, to say nothing of the master work *The Spirit of Mediaeval Philosophy*,[3] the Gifford Lectures delivered in 1931-1932 when the controversy had hardly begun. The problem of Christian Philosophy pervades the work of Gilson after 1931 and nothing less than a detailed and circumstantial discussion of his *oeuvre* could possibly do justice to his views. My intention here is far more modest.

I shall content myself with a number of *obiter dicta* on a distinction made by Jacques Maritain in his little book *De la philosophie chrétienne*,[4] published in 1933, and then go on to say a few things about the present status of Christian Philosophy in the United States.

Matters having to do with the adjective in the phrase "Christian philosophy" were, Maritain felt, better discussed with reference to the *state* of philosophy rather than its *nature*. Thus, to ask about the present status of Christian Philosophy is seemingly to embark upon an infinite regress—the state of the state, etc. Of course there is no real ambiguity here. Only a philosopher would have trouble with the wording of my task. Having proved that, if only glancingly, I pass on to the topic itself.

In the early Thirties, when Gilson and Maritain responded to the querulous claim of Bréhier that the concept of Christian Philosophy was incoherent, they quickly and rightly turned from Bréhier's pseudo-problem to issues that were their own and more important. The swiftest response to the charge was, *circumspice*, look around you. The Middle Ages provide us with numerous instances of Christian Philosophy. *Ab esse ad posse valet illatio. Ergo*, etc. Neither Maritain nor Gilson let it go at that, needless to say. Clearly the charge stirred up in them a desire to reflect on what they were doing as philosophers who were

Catholics. I want to recall very briefly what I take to be the abiding significance of what they had to say—it is because it is abiding that it fits under the title of our symposium—and then go on to characterize the philosophizing of Catholics in the United States today, with an added reference to the Society of Christian Philosophers formed just a few years ago.

The discussion of Christian Philosophy in the work of Maritain mentioned above moves on two levels, what I will call the modal and substantive levels.

> Indiquons tout de suite quel est pour nous le principe de la solution; c'est la distinction classique entre l'*ordre de spécification* et l'*ordre d'exercise*, ou encore, et c'est à ces termes que nous nous tiendrons, entre la nature et l'état.[5]

The modal level is captured by the distinction between nature and state, nature and condition, the order of specification and the order of exercise. It is not necessary to think of philosophy as some inert nature having properties of its own which is then carried around by various sweating Atlases whose itinerary is the basis for a number of *per accidens* remarks about their burden. Better to think of the activity of philosophizing—*philosophieren*, as Pieper puts it[6]—and to distinguish what characterizes it formally as such from what characterizes it as undertaken by so-and-so in such-and-such circumstances.

It is easy for us to see the kind of distinction involved in the case of the moral appraisal of a given act of thinking or philosophizing. The act of thinking is good if it achieves its end which is truth. But the act, thus appraised, may be appraised differently, and negatively, because of the circumstances in which it takes place. If I am lolling on my yacht devising sound and convincing proofs for the existence of God while ignoring the cries for help of drowning swimmers, it is clear that my thinking may receive a plus

or a minus depending on our point of view. A judgment of
the content of thought as opposed to a judgment of the
engagement in thinking by this concrete person here and
now, that is the distinction. Of course it would be odd and
otiose to respond to the statement "Whatever is moved is
moved by another" by asking "When? In the morning or
evening? In the Northern hemisphere as well as the
Southern?" By the same token, the schoolyard response,
"Who says so?" would be inappropriate. We might, of
course, want to make a similar distinction between sentences like "Roses are red" and "I have a toothache," saying that the latter but not the former involves the reporter
in the report and thus is differently appraised with regard
to its truth. But the distinction I am after is one that would
distinguish the intrinsic judgment of an act of thinking
(true or false?) from the moral judgment of it (good or
bad?).

For an act of thinking to be true is for it to be good in one
sense, but not in the moral sense. Just as it is not necessarily appropriate to utter any truth in just any circumstances
(to do so could be a sign of madness, gaucherie or breach
of promise, among other things), so the appraisal of an act
of thinking as true is not the end of the matter. Even remarks about roses are said by someone in particular circumstances and while we may agree that roses are red and
violets are blue, that does not settle whether the person
uttering these simple truths is also engaged in wooing,
translating from the Portuguese, encoding security information for the enemy, talking in his sleep or composing
a valentine that Hallmark will not buy.

It is best to make the distinction where there is conflict,
but of course it can happen that the act of thinking is
approved on both levels. The classical conception of philosophy presupposed that even theoretical thinking would
be, as well as the attainment of truth, a morally good activ-

ity. Indeed, one adumbration of the problem of Christian Philosophy in antiquity is the question as to whether a bad man could be a good philosopher, that is, the role of ethics in the philosophical life and the description of the philosophical ideal. It went without saying that the good ruler had to be a good man. How far we have come from that classical conception, even in the practical realm.

My suggestion, then, is that we can approach one facet of Maritain's handling of the question of Christian Philosophy by seeing the difference between a moral and an intrinsic appraisal of an act of theoretical thinking. Once we remind ourselves that the truth can be sought out of motives of vanity or the will to power or to *épater la bourgeoisie*, we can see how one might want so to describe the philosophical ideal as to insist that the right deed be done for the right reason and to suggest that without the appropriate moral orientation the whole thing is worthless. Plato held that it is moral virtue which gives us that necessary affinity with the really real which enables knowledge to take place. The elaboration of this *pathein/ mathein* view lifts the moral from mere modal status to a substantive feature of philosophizing.

One of the curiosities of the debate on Christian Philosophy that should not go unremarked, was the tendency of those who cast themselves in the role of defending *pure* philosophy to speak of Christians as if they alone came to the philosophical task with convictions and certainties. The notion of *pure* philosophy is a rich subject for comedy and no one had more fun with it than Kierkegaard. Pure Thought is thought without a thinker, and philosophers began to think of themselves as identified with this abstraction.[7] Unamuno, somewhat lugubriously, makes a similar point in *The Tragic Sense of Life* when he speaks of the man of flesh and bones. But of course theoretical thinking is merely one of the activities a man may engage in; not only can he not devote himself exclusively to it, in the life of even the most dedicated scholar it amounts to a small portion of his day. Getting from A to B, opening and shutting doors, lighting one's pipe, deciding to read this book or that, to write or think some more, on and on. There is a whole quotidian network that sustains and surrounds intellectual activity and without which it cannot be understood. That network includes implicit and explicit certainties about the world and ourselves and this has the quite unsurprising implication, save for some philosophers, that we *bring* truths to our philosophizing; not all knowledge is the *result* of philosophizing.

Needless to say, taking the quotidian network into account casts into an appropriately hilarious light the notion that philosophy should begin with doubt.

When philosophers have managed to expunge such home truths from their minds, they have fashioned wrong and dangerous conceptions of man. Thus, if one equates being a man, being human, with engaging in theoretical thinking of the most abstract kind, say, geometry, it would seem to follow from the fact that not even geometers do geometry most of the time that few men ever engage in the supposed specifically human activity. But what is to be said of all those activities humans engage in if they cannot be called human? Out of this exiguous picture of man came, inevitably, the bloodless moral philosophy we are only now beginning to free ourselves from.[8]

It is only when everyone engaged in the discussion stops talking about *pure* philosophy, in the sense of thought without a thinker, that it is possible to ask what is *peculiar* about what the Christian brings to the activity of philosophizing and how it differs from what others, e.g. secular humanists, bring to that task.[9] One of the peculiarities of the Roman Catholic philosopher, as witness this symposium, is that he takes with the utmost seriousness documents emanating from Rome and having to do with his activity, documents like the encyclical *Aeterni Patris*.

Docility to the Ordinary Magisterium has fallen on bad days, of course, with theologians seemingly eager to quibble with, distance themselves from or outrightly oppose Christ's vicar on earth. I prefer to direct my incredulity at such theologians and to rejoice in the fact that the Church has consistently and over many centuries put before the Catholic intellectual, particularly the philosopher and theologian, Saint Thomas Aquinas as a model. *Vae mihi si non thomistizavero*, Maritain wrote, and we might render it: For me not to follow Saint Thomas would be my ruin. That is the attitude we hope to see embodied in the Center whose inauguration we are celebrating. Anyone who thinks of that ideal as narrow or constraining need only consider the works of Etienne Gilson and Jacques Maritain. It was not merely one pope or one council or one committee that recommended Saint Thomas to us as a guide; it is the consistent and reiterated message of the Ordinary Magisterium. The only appropriate attitude toward this undeniable fact on the part of the Catholic is to see it as meant to help him attain the objectives of philosophy and theology. *Gustate et videte.*

This has to do with the starting point of our philosophizing. With what author should we begin? Any neophyte begins somewhere. Why does he begin where he does? The particular answers to that would be as numerous as the beginners but it seems fair enough to bring them all under one umbrella: one begins the study of philosophy where he does because he trusts someone. That is the common condition of the student. Viewed in this light, the situation of the Catholic is like anyone else's. But, of course, when he considers the authority and trustworthiness of *his* advisor, he can only conclude that he is in a far better position.

It is time that the Catholic intellectual resist the view that his existential situation is anomalous and in need of apology and adopt the more seemly stance of being grateful for the guidance he receives from the Church. The gift of faith is the best thing that ever happened to the human mind and the counsel and advice of those in whose keeping the deposit of faith is entrusted should be welcomed and received with joy, a joy which will eventually become a *gaudium de veritate*. It is silly to think that the upshot of all Catholics taking this advice will be uniformity and homogeneity of thinking. There is a single moral ideal for human persons which, if we pursue it seriously, will lead to a far greater differentiation among us rather than to somber sameness.

In the past several decades, interest in the thought of Saint Thomas has waned among Catholics even as it has waxed among our separated brethren. Doubtless there are dozens of reasons for this, few of them praiseworthy. Let us hope that the Center for Thomistic Studies here at the University of Saint Thomas will be a harbinger of a new renaissance of Thomism. Let us take up our all but discarded patrimony again and try to establish a mood like that which animated Etienne Gilson, Jacques Maritain, Charles De Koninck and Yves Simon, to speak only of those who came to us from abroad. Oh for the exuberance of a Chesterton, quoted to such effect by Pope John XXIII when he opened the Second Vatican Council! Those of us who have however fitfully and inadequately allowed our philosophizing to be guided by Saint Thomas Aquinas no longer merely believe that he is a good guide. It is something we have come to know. And that of course is the justification of the guidance. *Oportet addiscentem credere.* The complement of that truth is that, *in* philosophy, authority is the weakest argument.

So too Maritain, having provided a modal religious context within which philosophical thinking takes place, goes on to suggest that the objects of religious faith, believed truths, exercise an intrinsic influence on philosophical content, on philosophical truth. He does not want to say that the origin of a philosophical truth in a revealed truth—he takes creation as an example—means that the acceptance of this truth is always and everywhere dependent upon religious belief.

A few years ago we formed the Society of Christian Philosophers, a group that holds regional meetings—these have been held at the University of Notre Dame as well as at Wheaton College in Illinois—and national meetings in conjunction with the eastern meeting of the American Philosophical Association.

It is a welcome thing to have philosophers identify themselves as Christians and, by doing so, to suggest that this has significance for them as philosophers. By and large, the non-Catholic membership in the Society consists of Evangelicals and Calvinists and Lutherans. Not surprisingly, when one considers the dominant themes of recent Philosophy of Religion, a central theme of the society is that religious belief is a rational, a reasonable activity to engage in. What I want to draw attention to, by way of contrast to what such a claim would mean in the context of *Aeterni Patris*, is the minimalistic, not to say fideistic, flavor of the thought of many of my colleagues in the Society.

If one maintains that belief is reasonable in the sense that no one can successfully convict the believer of inconsistency, contradiction, or some other mode of irrationality, this is not nothing. Oftentimes this position takes the form of a So's your old man argument. A classical instance of this can be found in Alvin Plantinga's *God and Other Minds*. The upshot of the book is that it is no less reasonable to assert the existence of God than it is to assert the existence of other minds. This does not come down to any direct assertion that it is reasonable to affirm the existence of God. The technique of the book has led to the neologism "to alvinize." One alvinizes when, confronted by an attack on religious belief, one responds by seeking and finding a tenet of the attacker that can be shown to be at least as suspect, on the attacker's grounds, as the claims of religious belief. The *tu quoque* or *ad hominem* flavor of this is at once its appeal and its limitation.

In the same book, Plantinga examines versions of traditional proofs for the existence of God and finds them wanting. The suggestion thus is that while nothing positive can be rationally established with respect to theism, insofar as theism has problems they are shared by many convictions that the antitheist (Plantinga's atheologist) would be most reluctant to relinquish.

If Plantinga is typical of the Society—a pleasant thought since he is one of the most gifted philosophers and one of the most edifying Calvinists I know—it would be fair to say that fideism is rampant in the Society of Christian Philosophers. The status of Christian Philosophy should be discussed, I think, with particular reference to the status of natural theology. Traditionally understood, the reasonableness of belief is a claim that has reposed on an interpretation of Romans 1:19-20 which has it that men are capable, independently of faith, of arriving at knowledge of the invisible things of God. This is a task which cannot be ignored. Techniques such as alvinizing are useful and good and we should be grateful for them. But to settle for them would be to abandon one of the essential features of Christian Philosophy, viz. that there are sound and valid proofs of God's existence and of other *praeambula fidei* and that this provides a basis for the argument that it is reasonable to accept the *mysteria fidei* as true.

At the risk of unction of the extremer sort, let me conclude by drawing attention to a little book that Maritain authored with his wife Raïssa, *Prayer and Intelligence.*[10] As in Maritain's greatest work, *Les degrés du savoir*, the smaller work, originally titled *La vie d'Oraison*, reminds us that just as the ethical provides a wider context in which the activity of theoretical thinking can be appraised, so too does religion. God did not become man in order that men might become theologians. Contemplation, the fulfillment of the spiritual life, is the common supernatural goal of human persons. It is no less the goal of the Christian philosopher. Just as there has been an unhappy dissociation of thought and life, so there can be in the believer a dissociation of thought and the spiritual life. Saint Thomas, we remember, began study with a prayer and his study thus became a species of prayer. It is not without significance that the patron of Catholic intellectual life is a saint. Bloy's adage still obtains. There is only one tragedy, not to become a saint. How many saintly philosophers do you know? That is a judgment on us. The deepest significance of the notion of Christian Philosophy is that it would have us avoid a tragic life in this sense.

1. Maurice Nédoncelle, *Is There A Christian Philosophy?* Twentieth Century Encyclopedia of Catholicism (New York: Hawthorn Books, 1960), pp. 85-99.

2. In *Philosophies Chrétiennes*, Recherches et Débats (Paris: Librairie Fayard, 1955), pp. 35-68.

3. Translated by A.H.C. Downes (New York: Scribner's, 1940). *Christianisme et Philosophie* (Paris: Vrin, 1949); *Introduction à la philosophie chrétienne* (Paris; Vrin, 1960). *The Philosopher and Theology* (New York: Random House, 1962).

4. Paris: Desclée de Brouwer, 1933).

5. Ibid., p. 27.

6. Josef Pieper, *Was heisst philosophieren?* (Munich: Hegner, 1948).

7. Søren Kierkegaard, *Concluding Unscientific Postscript.*

8. See Iris Murdoch, *The Sovereignty of the Good.*

9. See my *Thomism in an Age of Renewal* (New York: Doubleday, 1966).

10. (New York: Sheed and Ward, 1938).

Thomism and Today's Crisis in Moral Values

Michael Bertram Crowe

University College, Dublin

There can hardly be any doubt about the existence of a crisis of moral values in the world today. There have been such crises before. The Roman Empire in its decline presented a situation critical for moral values; likewise the emergence of secularism in the eighteenth century. Our age, this latter half of the twentieth century, seems very conscious of such precedents—and commonly describes itself as a period in which moral values face a crisis. There is notably an awareness of a new moral permissiveness. Our society recognizes itself as the 'permissive society'; and permissiveness has recently been defined as:

> the view that the individual's pursuit of pleasure should, provided no harm is done to others, be unrestricted by external factors such as laws or by internal guilt arising from social conventions. The *permissive society*, a cliché of the late 1960s, is exemplified by the decline of stage and film censorship, by public acquiescence in the relaxation of certain moral and social conventions, and by recent legislation concerning adult consenting homosexuals, abortion, divorce and what constitutes pornography...[1]

We are here, however, less concerned with what might be

described as the *praxis* of permissiveness than with the *theoria* (or lack of it) that brings it about. Taking the fact of a declension in moral values for granted we look for its cause or causes.

We look first to the philosophical influence upon the decline of moral values—and here it must be simply a question of listing some of the philosophical positions and attitudes that have shaped the modern mind. Evolutionist philosophies, exempting nothing from the process of change, not even cultural or moral values, have made it impossible to assign a fixed or permanent basis for value-judgments. Scientific humanism, the contemporary and more sophisticated variant of nineteenth century evolutionism, with the addition of elements from psychology, has reinforced this same result; Darwin's undermining of moral values compounded by Freud. Logical positivism— the early Ayer, popularizing the views of the Wiener Kreis—emptied moral judgments of meaning. If meaning attaches only to statements that are either tautologous or can be empirically verified, then moral propositions do not qualify as statements. Their only function is that of communicators and fomentors of feeling or emotion, a view for which the considerable authority of David Hume can be invoked. It is a far cry from traditional expositions of moral philosophy, which believe moral propositions to be both meaningful and capable of demonstration. A second prong of the logical positivist attack lies in the 'is-ought' difficulty, adverted to (although in a passing way) in David Hume's *Treatise of Human Nature* and prominent in twentieth century moral philosophy, particularly that written in English. If one accepts that to proceed from judgments of fact ('is') to judgments of value ('ought') necessarily involves a fallacy, then moral values seem to be compromised. Again Marxism or dialectical materialism, asserting that moral values, like all other values, are part of a

superstructure and merely reflect the changing economic
forces that determine human society, rules out what we
must call the traditional understanding of moral philosophy. Lastly, existentialism—or its outgrowth, situation-
ethics—shows perhaps the most direct attack upon moral
values; for situationism, at least in its extreme form, denies
the possibility of moral principles.

These varieties of philosophy are undoubtedly among
the factors contributing to the current crisis of moral
values. But what precisely is it that is threatened by them?
The answer might be given in two words: the Categorical
Imperative. Or, if we wish to spell it out somewhat, it is
the transcendence of moral over other values, utilitarian,
cultural, biological, monetary and so on. If the Categorical
Imperative appears too Kantian, or seems to imply that
duty was not recognized before Kant, then we may be
content simply to look at the notion of moral good. Ob-
ligatoriness, however expressed, seems an integral part of
moral goodness; and the implication is easily seen that
moral goodness must have a certain universality, so that
what is good (or of obligation) for me must similarly be
good for any other individual in my circumstances. 'Circumstances' and 'same circumstances' are, of course, ideas
that will demand close analysis. But the problem posed by
our contemporary situation is: How can we, in the climate,
—moral, philosophical, permissive—of today, formulate
general or universal principles about the good and the obligation it imposes upon us? Indeed, it is not a single problem but a cluster of problems. When we generalize—
formulate a principle or a norm of action—we are doing
something that, traditionally, moral philosophy has
always done. Our present difficulty lies in attempting to
justify such generalization—not, admittedly, a new difficulty, but one that has today a pressing urgency. Whether
there is in morals such a thing as an absolute statement, a

principle admitting of no exception, is a question that is being asked more and more insistently.

The question has been much discussed. A well-known essay of Paul Ramsey, written some years ago, "The Case of the Curious Exception," is a case in point.[2] Can a moral principle be formulated in such a way that it admits of no exception? Can qualifications be built into a principle, such as that about not killing, so that it obliges irrespective of circumstances, so that in no conceivable situation is it not of obligation? Without entering into the detail of that discussion we can, I believe, recognize the same problematic in our present topic: What, if anything, has Thomism to offer in the current crisis of moral values?

Here we may be helped by a brief consideration of the main controversies in Christian theological ethics, notably in the work of Catholic thinkers, over the past few decades. If we cast our minds back to the end of the Second World War and the 1950s we find that, for Catholic moralists, the main area of controversy had to do with existentialist or situation ethics. By the 1960s the emphasis had moved to the question of the impact of moral philosophy on political and social questions. In the 1970s the debate was mainly about the Christian ethic: What is it that, specifically, Christianity gives to moral philosophy? In what way is moral philosophy different for the Christian? Is there an autonomous moral philosophy and what should be the Christian's attitude towards it? Such questions forced many Christian writers to explore the nature of moral philosophy more closely than they had hitherto done, with a view to understanding what additional modality Christianity gives to it—if this, in fact, is what Christian revelation does. Today, however, the issue has become more concrete and more fundamental: What, after all, do we mean by moral law? and: Can absolute norms be justified? May I suggest that all these controversies and

areas of dispute are basically the same and that this last
formulation, the question of the foundation of moral law,
epitomizes them all?

Are there absolute norms in ethics? Over a decade ago
Charles Curran edited a book entitled: *Absolutes in Moral
Theology?*[3] It is no criticism to say that publication did not
remove the question mark of the title; for the problem is
still with us and will remain. It is the issue to which we
must address ourselves, not simply because we see it to be
the central issue in domestic controversies of Catholic
moralists and others, but because it goes to the very heart
of the current crisis of moral values, questioning, as it
does, the very nature of moral philosophy.

Let us look at two contexts in which the centrality of this
issue appears. Firstly, let us examine the proposition that
the end does not justify the means, a commonplace, one
might say, of moral philosophy and moral theology. The
acceptance of this proposition implies that there are some
means that no end can justify, in other words, that there
are some human actions that can absolutely or uncondi-
tionally be characterized as evil. Whether they are described as 'intrinsically' or *'per se'* or *'secundum se'* evil or
with any other terminological nuance, need not detain us
for the moment. The fact is that such actions, the killing of
the innocent for instance, are assumed to be evil in such a
way or to such a degree that no good purpose or intention
could justify them. Suppose that, in a given situation, the
direct killing of one innocent person would save the lives
of twenty others. If the morality of the killing depends
solely upon the consequences, it become difficult to see
any reason for refraining. This is the often-discussed case
of the Southern sheriff who, in a riot situation following
upon the rape of a white woman, ensures the judicial
murder of one negro, who is innocent, in order to avoid
more deaths. That such is not merely an hypothetical case

was seen in the controversy, some years ago, surrounding the nomination of Auxiliary Bishop-elect Defregger of Munich. For, as a German officer serving in Italy during the Second World War, Defregger had been implicated in the shooting of hostages as a reprisal for a partisan attack. What he did had the net result of saving lives that would otherwise have been lost (for the number to be shot was reduced); and the killing of innocent people could not have been prevented in any case. Nevertheless what he did— and abstracting from the question of personal culpability— was regarded by many as objectively or intrinsically evil. It was a means that the good end could not justify.

Many similar cases are adduced in the existentialist and situationist literature of our time; indeed they tend to be repeated from one author to the next.

> On the Wilderness Trail, Daniel Boone's trail westward through Cumberland Gap to Kentucky, many families in the trail caravan lost their lives to the Indians. A Scottish woman had a baby at the breast. The baby was ill and crying, and the baby's crying was betraying her other three children and the rest of the party...the mother clung to the baby; the baby's cries led the Indians to the position; and the party was discovered and all were massacred. There was another such occasion. On this occasion there was a Negro woman in the party. Her baby too was crying and threatening to betray the party. She strangled the baby with her own two hands to stop its crying—and the whole party escaped.[4]

A case, the same in all essentials, was reported in a book, published by the Israeli Defence Ministry, Yitzhak Nimtsovitz's *Because of Them*. A certain Mr. Kramer had built a bunker near his home at Dolhinov, near Vilna. The Germans were hunting Jews in the village and shooting

them at sight. A total of forty-seven Jews were concealed
in the bunker, including Mr. Kramer, his wife Genia and
their son David. As the Germans approached the house,
the baby suddenly started wailing. All eyes turned to Mr.
Kramer, who hesitated for a long, anguished moment and
then strangled his son. All of the Jews in the bunker escaped.[5] Did this end justify the means?

One further example of the moral dilemma may be
offered. St. Augustine recalls an incident alleged to have
taken place at Antioch about 345 A.D. The prefect of the
district, Acindinus, had imprisoned a man for debt and
threatened to execute him. The man had a very beautiful
wife, much desired by a rich man who offered to pay the
debt in return for favors of her bed for one night. Having
consulted her husband, the wife submitted. And Augustine's assessment of the situation is far from censorious.
The husband, he says, did not regard as adultery what was
done, not out of libidiousness but out of love. (*"nullo
modo...adulterium esse concubitum quod et libido nulla et magna
mariti charitas se jubente et volente flagitaret...non ita respuit
hoc sensus humanus quod in illa muliere, viro jubente, com-
missum est.*[6] This is also the situation in Shakespeare's
Measure for Measure, where Isabella makes it clear that she
will not save her brother from execution by sleeping with
the duke of Vienna's deputy.

Joseph Fletcher, in his *Situation Ethics*, gives the twentieth-century version. As the Russian armies drove west-
ward to meet the Americans and British at the Elbe, a
Soviet patrol picked up a Mrs. Bergmeier, foraging for
food for her three children. She was taken off to a prison
camp in the Ukraine. Meanwhile her husband had been
captured in the Bulge and taken to a POW camp in Wales.
On his release he traced the three children; but their
mother's whereabouts remained a mystery.

Meanwhile, in the Ukraine, Mrs. Bergmeier learned

through a sympathetic commandant that her husband and family were trying to keep together and find her. But the rules allowed them to release her for only two reasons: (1) illness needing medical facilities beyond the camp's, in which case she would be sent to a Soviet hospital elsewhere, and (2) pregnancy, in which case she would be returned to Germany as a liability.

She turned things over in her mind and finally asked a friendly Volga German camp guard to impregnate her, which he did. Her condition being medically verified, she was sent back to Berlin and to her family. They welcomed her with open arms even when she told them how she managed it. When the child was born they loved him more than all the rest, on the view that little Dietrich had done more for them than anybody.[7]

So much, for the moment, about end and means. Let us look at the second context in which the question of the possibility of moral absolutes is seen to be critical. There has been much discussion, over the past ten years, of the so-called Principle of the Double Effect, or Principle of Mixed Results. When one wills an action, one is normally presumed to intend its foreseen results. But the results of human action are frequently multiple and include some that are wanted and desired and others that are not desired but merely tolerated, or, as the terminology has it, indirectly intended. The Principle of the Double Effect is the moralists' summary of the conditions under which they consider an undesirable effect, such as the death of the innocent, might be tolerated, that is, indirectly willed, in a complex situation. The implication is not far to seek that there are some such effects that may never be directly intended—indirect permission or toleration (whose niceties we need not here enter into) is the limit of what is morally allowable. Were the same effect to be directly procured, so the argument runs, the action would be evil. This is an issue that greatly exercises contemporary moralists: Franz Scholz, Bruno Schüller, Josef Fuchs, Louis Janssens, Germain Grisez, William Van der Marck, Paul Ramsey, Richard McCormick and many others. The Principle of the Double Effect has been familiar in the field of medical ethics, more particularly over the last fifty years. And now that the problems of medicine and of bioethics have become so complex and so far-reaching in their implications, the principle has come in for very close scrutiny. And the scrutiny brings into the sharpest focus the difference between the tendency to judge morality on the basis of the consequences of an act ('consequentialism', '*Güterabwegung*') and the insistence upon the absoluteness of at least some moral precepts.

For some moralists, of course, the solution in ends-means or double-effect contexts lies ready to hand. For a situationist like Joseph Fletcher "only the end justifies the means, nothing else."[8] For a Marxist, all means that lead to the success of the final revolution are justified. For many, and not merely positivists or humanists, there are no actions that can be ruled out in advance of the consideration of their results in a given situation. In particular, the double-effect problematic arises precisely because it is taken that some actions can be categorized, in advance of choice, as evil (and therefore as not to be directly intended). Josef Fuchs, among others, meets this by drawing attention to the fact that no action, in advance of human intention, can be more than physical or 'ontic' evil; moral evil or wickedness requires that it should be intended.[9] We can, perhaps, restate the problem by asking whether there are not some objects of choice which, if they are chosen, inevitably constitute evil in the totality of the action. Take for example the death of an innocent party. In advance of someone's willing it, this can be described as evil only in the sense in

which a death in a landslide or an earthquake is evil—
physical, 'ontic' or 'pre-moral' evil. But may one choose
directly to kill an innocent person?

What can Thomism offer in this crisis of moral values? It
is hardly necessary to say that the quarrying of suitable
texts from the works of St. Thomas, with a disregard for
chronology and the development of his thought and in
ignorance of his historical sources, is unlikely to be helpful. If Thomism is to have anything to offer, it must be a
sound and defensible Thomism and not a travesty of the
thought of Aquinas divorced from its historical setting.
One must follow the example of modern interpreters of St.
Thomas, like Pierre Mandonnet or Odon Lottin, who
looked at what St. Thomas said and saw it in its historical
circumstances. Thomas must be seen *in textu et contextu*—
which means not merely the literary context but above all
the philosophical-theological-historical context. Only thus
can we sift what is perennial in his thought—and, so, likely
to help us today—from what is conditioned by his age and
his culture. What do we have from Aquinas to bring to the
question of moral values?

To begin with, we have a basic anthropology, a conception of human nature which is the underpinning of morality. The phrase 'human nature' can be highly ambiguous;
and Thomas' appeal to it has been presented in a simplistic
way. In reality his concept of human nature is far more
complex and far more flexible than is often assumed. It
should not be forgotten that he did say, upon occasion,
that human nature is changeable (*natura humana mutabilis
est*).[10] He also had a good deal to say about the flexibility
and variability of moral reasonings, which would belie the
rigid conclusions often foisted upon him in the name of
human nature. As a good Aristotelian, he recognized that
in moral matters one cannot look for the kind of demonstrations and certainty appropriate to the speculative

sciences. (*In negotiis humanis non potest haberi demonstrativa probatio et infallibilis; sed sufficit aliqua conjecturalis probabilitas.*[11]) These assertions are less startling when seen in their context. For Aquinas is not talking about unchanging abstract nature, but about human nature concretely exemplified in the individual, who finds himself in a particular historical and cultural situation in which his fellow-men play an inescapable part. Aquinas would hardly accept Sartre's suggestion that human nature is what we make ourselves; but he might have considerable sympathy for Rahner's notion of man's nature in a process of development to which man himself contributes.

Secondly, Thomism offers an analysis of human action in which the important moral dimensions are singled out. There is no need here to rehearse the well-known doctrine of the moral determinants, the object, the circumstances and the intention of the action—beyond saying that it is not quite as simple as it has occasionally been made to appear. Here, certainly, we ought to judge St. Thomas on his own text and its context, rather than in the often impoverished expositions still sometimes found. When Thomas stresses the fundamental importance of the object, with all that follows concerning 'objective' morality, we should recall that he is not saying that it is the exclusive determinant of morality. He makes play with the Dionysian principle: *Bonum ex integra causa, malum ex quocunque defectu.*[12] All elements, in an action no less than in a thing, must be integral if the totality is to be good; if defect is found in any element then, by definition, the whole is defective. A moral action can be defective in its object, in its circumstances or in its intention. And if contemporary moral philosophy is tempted to stress intention, to the exclusion of the other two determinants, we should not assume that Thomas adopts the opposite extreme of fixing upon the object to the exclusion of the others. He takes all three determinants, as he was bound to do by the logic of the Dionysian principle about goodness; and he gives due prominence to intention by suggesting that it is related to object and circumstances more or less as form is to matter.[13]

This is not to undervalue the importance—the radical importance—of the object. If an action, in what it directly achieves, i.e. in its object, is defective, then it cannot be healed or cured of its lack of integrity by circumstances that are sympathetic or an intention that is laudable. Of which actions may it be said that their object is of this kind—that, indeed, is another question. Aquinas adverts to it when he says (it is only one example) that murder is murder: *Homicidium est occisio innocentis et hoc nullo modo bene fieri potest.*[14] Everyone knows that killing cannot be said to be in itself evil; there are justifiable homicides. But the killing of the innocent is in a different category; can it ever be a good action? Recently John Dedek[15] has made a study of this 'intrinsic morality' or 'objective morality' not merely in St. Thomas but in his predecessors. He points out that what Thomas held was what had been held, with some minor variations, by his predecessors from the beginning of the thirteenth century at Paris. Certain actions like lying, killing the innocent, stealing, were characterized as in themselves evil and therefore incapable of being morally good, even if done for a good purpose or in beneficial circumstances. But closer inspection reveals the tautologies here. It amounts to saying that unlawful killing cannot be lawful or that adultery is wrong because it is the unjust violation of another's rights. The actions, thus formally identified in their moral import, cannot be justified without contradiction. But St. Thomas, no less than his predecessors and contemporaries, was perfectly aware that the material actions, killing or taking property, are not always wrong. His views must be carefully studied and interpreted—and not simply used to pre-empt positions in the contemporary discussions about morality.

If there is one central concept in the moral teaching of Aquinas, a focus for his thinking on moral matters, it is arguably the natural law. This doctrine, too, must be taken in its text and context. One must study not alone what Thomas himself says, in the chronological order of his writing from the first tentative outlines to the final synthesis, but also what his predecessors had said, for there was an extensive literature on the topic, with which he was familiar. As for the long and tortuous history of the natural law, as reflected in that literature, we may confine our consideration here to two landmarks. There are two definitions, embodying, one might say, two approaches, to the natural law that had achieved notoriety in the authors when St. Thomas came to write in the thirteenth century. The first is the definition, ascribed to the Roman jurist Ulpian and found at the head of the *Corpus Juris Civilis*: natural law is what nature has taught all animals. Thomas, we may think surprisingly, accepted this definition. Writing, as he did in the mid-thirteenth century, it was not really open to him to reject out of hand a definition that was invested with the august majesty of the Roman law. Albert the Great, it may be said in passing, was not so squeamish and was prepared to say that there cannot be a genuine law common to man and animals. Aquinas said the same, but more subtly. He accepted the definition only to interpret it; and his interpretation went a long way towards making Ulpian conform to a notion of a natural law based upon human reason. Whether this can be done in an altogether consistent way is another question.

The second definition that passed to Aquinas with authority was that of the canonists. In the mid-twelfth century Gratian, in his *Decretum*, which in its way was as authoritative for canon law as the *Corpus* of Justinian was for the Roman law, defined the natural law as what is contained in the Law and the Gospel. There is, of course, a sense in which this is true; but there is also a sense in which the definition can be described (as it was by Dom Lottin) as an egregious confusion between divine or revealed law and the natural law discoverable to man's reason. Once again Thomas was not really free, in the circumstances in which he wrote, to say outright that Gratian and his distinguished commentators were wrong on the matter. But he was perfectly free to do as he did, to accept the definition and to re-interpret it, shaping it to his own purposes. Matters of this sort are, clearly, of the greatest importance in understanding the thought of Aquinas. In his handling of these definitions we can see the direction in which his thought is moving; we can glimpse his definitive view of the natural law.

Natural law, for St. Thomas, the law of human nature, is essentially connected with the rationality that is the specific character of human nature. The natural law is the law of reason; the good action is the reasonable action, the evil what is contrary to reason. Reason is afforded some indicators from the material and biological dimensions in human existence; or, to use the terminology of the famous question in the *Prima Secundae*,[16] the rational nature of man has much to learn from the nature he shares with animals and the nature he shares with all substances. But the overriding consideration remains that the good action is the one that conforms to man's rational nature. The relevance of this consideration for contemporary controversies about use and abuse of the human generative faculty will not be lost. Sufficient to say here that St. Thomas must not be made to support the view of a purely biological criterion of morality, in this or in any other sphere. His view of human nature is quite capable of accommodating developments and qualifications, demanded by the contemporary crisis—

without abandoning the proposition that morality is written in human nature.

The argument that some actions, like contraception, are to be rejected because they violate the biological structure of human existence, is, at best, an incomplete and inconclusive argument. Apart from the evident fact that we frequently violate the biological structure of actions—as when, for therapeutic reasons, we take medicines such as emetics, or, for aesthetic or cultural reasons, we shave our beards,—there is the more important consideration that the 'biological act' is not a coherent term if it is used to mean the kind of act we can qualify as good or evil. The biological is necessarily pre-rational, non-rational. If the argument is rescued by suggesting that the biological structure must be respected by the reason (or will) that freely posits the act in question, then the question must be asked (and it is implicit in Thomas): What constitutes reasonable respect for biology? The essential matter to be decided, here as elsewhere, is: What is it reasonable to do in the circumstances?

In the discussion of questions such as these, Thomism does have a great deal to offer, despite the fact that they were unknown in the thirteenth century. What is needed—and it seems to be found in Thomism—is a way of securing the objectivity of morality, with human nature as the criterion of morality and the foundation of the natural moral law, and at the same time the taking into account of the living, dynamic aspect of morality, not settled once and for all, but having within itself possibilities of adaptation and change.

Finally, the summary of St. Thomas' magnificent synthesis of natural law teaching must include epistemological considerations. Natural law is formulated in a series of rational principles. And here we return to where we began, to the problem of generalization in ethics. For

Aquinas there are moral principles which, in moral reasonings, play the part played, in reasoning processes in general, by the first principles of thought, sometimes called logical first principles. These moral principles, the beginning and the end of moral discourse, as the principles of identity or of non-contradiction are the beginning and end of rational discourse, are otherwise described by St. Thomas as the first precepts of the natural law. They are allied to human nature, as rational; they provide the criterion of morality. They, with their hinterland of teaching just outlined, encapsulate the positive and pervasive contribution of Thomas to the contemporary crisis in moral values.

1. *The Fontana Dictionary of Modern Thought*, ed. Allan Bullock and Oliver Stallybrass (London, 1977), p. 465.

2. *Norm and Context in Christian Ethics*, ed. G.H. Outka and P. Ramsey, (New York: Scribner's, 1968), pp. 67-135,

3. *Absolutes in Moral Theology*, ed. Charles Curran (Washington-Cleveland: Corpus Books, 1968).

4. W. Barclay, *Ethics in a Permissive Society*, (London: Collins-Fontana, 1971), p. 71.

5. Report in *Jerusalem Post Weekly*, (December 7, 1971).

6. *De sermone Domini in Monte*, I, xvi, 50, Migne, *Patrologia Latina*, 34: 1254.

7. (London: SCM Press, 1966), Appendix, pp. 164-165, "Sacrificial Adultery."

8. *Situation Ethics*, p. 120.

9. Josef Fuchs, "The Absoluteness of Moral Terms," *Gregorianum*, 52 (1971): 442-447.

10. *ST*, II-II, 57, 2 ad 1; *De malo*, 2, 4 ad 13; *In IV Sent.*, d. 26, q. 1, a. 1 ad 3; d. 33, q. 1, a. 2 ad 1.

11. *ST*, I-II, 105, 2 ad 8.

12. *ST*, I-II, 18, 4 ad 3.

13. Cf. *ST*, I-II, 18, 6.

14. *ST*, I, 88, 6.

15. In *The Thomist*, 43 (1979): 385-413.

16. *ST*, I-II, 94, 2.

Transcendental Thomism
A Critical Assessment

Robert J. Henle, S.J.

Saint Louis University

I do not intend in this paper to give a balanced or comprehensive assessment of the "School" or "Movement" known as Transcendental Thomism. Some of the most brilliant Catholic thinkers of the last fifty years have either practiced the transcendental method or been deeply influenced by the movement.[1] The writings of these men contain many profound philosophical reflections and some enduring contributions to the cumulative goods of philosophy.[2] But as Paul Elmer More once remarked, genius is no guarantee against error. It is, therefore, with the utmost respect for these men that I present here a deliberately negative critique of Transcendental Thomism. Moreover, I do not pretend that this presentation is complete and final. It is a brief preliminary statement of my own position vis-a-vis Transcendental Thomism—a position which I hope subsequently to develop and, if necessary, correct.

The denial that Joseph Maréchal founded a "school" seems to be based on the fact that individual thinkers have tried to carry out his original projection in very personal and different ways.[3] This fact has persuaded me to deal with the movement selectively, both in the authors studied and in the points emphasized.

The historical and doctrinal starting point is obviously the work of Joseph Maréchal (1878-1944) and the Magna

90

Carta of the movement is his brilliant *Le Point de départ de la métaphysique*.[4] Since he laid down the guidelines for the Thomistic use of the Transcendental Method, an understanding of Maréchal is essential to the understanding of any further development thereof. I will therefore make considerable use of his work. But my approach is bipolar and at the other pole I have selected Emerich Coreth, the distinguished German exponent of the Transcendental Method. Several considerations have guided my selection. First of all, it seems to me that Emerich Coreth does indeed lie within the authentic development of the "movement" with, however, the reservations to be mentioned later. Secondly, he presents in his *Metaphysik* a total and systematic metaphysics—"Eine Methodisch-Systematische Grundlegung" worked out, according to his express intention by the exclusive use of the Transcendental Method.[5] Though the work is long and profound, it is almost a basic textbook in metaphysics according to a Transcendental Method. I know of no other Transcendental Thomist who has made an effort to present a total metaphysics in such a systematic form. Father Donceel has produced in English a condensed translation of this work intended obviously to be used as a college textbook in the United States. Maréchal proposed to use the Transcendental Method as an alternative method and a roundabout modern way to arrive at the already existing metaphysical realism of St. Thomas.[6] One might then expect to find in Coreth's *Metaphysik*, some fifty years later, a systematic fulfillment of Maréchal's purpose.

I am deliberately leaving Bernard Lonergan outside my discussion except insofar as he comments on Coreth.[7] Lonergan seems to me to have antecedents other than those in the transcendental tradition and to have distinctive philosophical views which cannot be reduced to that tradition, however much they may converge with it.[8] He is, of course, of great importance in modern Catholic thought, but he deserves an individual and distinctive critique. Indeed some of what I say of the Maréchal-Coreth axis will apply to him, but I will not make the application here.

To return to Coreth there is another more profound and philosophical reason for selecting him as the current representative of the movement. He seems to me to represent, if not the logical terminus, at least the penultimate stage in the logical working out of the use of the Transcendental Method in accordance with Maréchal's original program. Gilson has shown how philosophical systems and doctrines develop not merely through history but in accordance with philosophical principles.[9] From this standpoint I believe that Coreth represents almost the final separation of Transcendental Thomism from Thomism under the intrinsic pressure of principles alien to Thomism and to metaphysical realism. Coreth represents the historical devolution of the movement to its historical demise.[10] It can only survive now as a Christianized version of German idealism.

Obviously, from Maréchal and throughout the history of the movement, the crucial issue has been that of the methodology of metaphysics, the so-called "transcendental turn."[11] We can, indeed, measure the distance travelled from Maréchal to Coreth by examining their conceptions of the role and function of the Transcendental Method.

Maréchal held that there was already in existence a perfectly sound metaphysical realism established by a methodology that was both natural and correct. He did not propose to modify the metaphysics of knowledge or the metaphysical realism of St. Thomas Aquinas. The existence of this metaphysics as valid was a given in his approach to the problem.[12] However, he thought that for purposes of revalidating the Thomistic synthesis within modern philosophy and in the face of the so-called "modern" problematic the method first developed by Kant and called by him "transcendental" could be so modified that, starting with it, one could arrive at the already given metaphysics of St. Thomas.[13] In other words, Maréchal saw two methodologies by which the same metaphysics might be established.[14] He did not propose to modify the traditional methodology of Thomism at all or to substitute another methodology for it. But he was convinced that the Kantian Transcendental Method could be corrected and used in such a way as to overcome Kantianism and establish Thomism, thereby beating Kant at his own game.

If we turn now to Coreth we find no longer an acceptance of two methodologies. Coreth sees the transcendental method as the *only* legitimate method for establishing a metaphysics; there are no alternative ways.[15] The approval and defense of the natural approach of traditional Thomism is completely discarded. The adoption of the transcendental method is not seen as an intellectual strategy nor as a means of bringing Thomism into modern thought but as establishing, for the first time, a thoroughgoing valid metaphysics.[16]

Coreth's general conception of methodology is such that there can be only *one* proper methodology for each discipline.[17] He sees methodology as intimately associated with whatever discipline it is related to. The nature of the investigation determines the methodology to be used and the methodology that is used determines the nature of the discipline as it develops.[18] It seems to me that Coreth's view in this matter is absolutely right. The methodological principles as well as the starting points of any discipline determine its character and its conclusions, and its character and its conclusions must be understood and interpreted in terms of the argumentation, both with regard to the initial substantive position and with regard to the mode of argumentation, the methodology itself.

This view of methodology was expressly developed by St. Thomas, not only in his general epistemological doctrine on the division of the disciplines but especially in his clear and fundamental distinction between the *Via Platonica* and the *Via Aristotelis*.[19] He understood that a position derived its meaning from its premises or from the general mode—the *via*—of the argumentation. Two methodologies could lead to a common position only equivocally.

If then Coreth is correct in his theory of the relationship of any methodology to its corresponding discipline one would expect that whatever methodology he selected for metaphysics would, in his opinion at least, be the one and only proper methodology. This is exactly what Coreth says with regard to the Transcendental Method. There is only one metaphysical method, the Transcendental Method. Furthermore, if Coreth is correct then Maréchal's assumption that there could be two basically different methodologies by which the same metaphysical positions could be established has to be rejected. As a consequence of this it also follows that if one adopts the Transcendental Method as the one and only method to do metaphysics then one would expect that the resultant metaphysics would be different from the metaphysics established by a prior and different methodology.

It is my contention that this is exactly the outcome of the movement. When new principles are introduced into a given tradition the first impact may not be pervasive or profound. The full implications of the new principles, the full influence of the new methodologies may not be originally worked out or even suspected. What we have seen so far in the development from Maréchal to Coreth is the working out of the substitution of an alien methodology within the Thomistic tradition in the hope that the same body of metaphysical knowledge will be thereby established. On the contrary, this cannot be done and has not happened. What we have now in Coreth's metaphysics is not a Thomism but a kind of Christianized transcendentalism, or an idealism corrected by Christian realism.

While earlier Transcendental Thomists were very insistent that they were arriving at the authentic metaphysics of St. Thomas and that they were reestablishing his basic positions it has become clear to the more recent exponents of the position that this is not the case.

Thus, it is very significant that one of the most distinguished members of the movement, Karl Rahner, has expressly recognized this fact. In his introduction to Muck's work on Transcendental Method he writes, "The author discusses the Transcendental Method in contemporary '*scholastic* philosophy,' i.e., he sketches the history of the reception of a mode of thought which so alters the recepting 'system' that it becomes an entirely new and different one. The reception of the Transcendental Method means the end of 'neo-scholasticism' in the historical sense of the word."[20] Further on he adds, "Nor does the transcendental turn mean merely the adoption of a brand new doctrine in an otherwise stable and static 'system,' but an entirely new conception of the 'system' itself. This is what leads us to speak confidently of the end of neo-scholasticism as it had been understood since the second half of the nineteenth century."[21]

I do not believe that the continued validity of neo-scholasticism or of Thomism or their future redevelopment, stands or falls with Transcendental Thomism. But I think that it is quite clear that at this point Transcendental Thomism can no longer claim to be Thomism and that some of its major exponents are recognizing this fact. Moreover, the failure of the Transcendental Method to carry out the program of Maréchal is, in my opinion, being demonstrated by history and one of the major demonstrations is the *Metaphysik* of Coreth.

It is not surprising therefore to discover that Coreth himself puts the development of his metaphysics and especially of his methodology in the line of Kant-Fichte-Schelling-Hegel and a group of modern philosophers that includes Husserl and Heidegger.[22] It is to this "Richtung" that Coreth attaches his development of the Transcendental Method. He mentions as antecedents, if not as sources, the neo-scholastics Maréchal, G. Isaye, J.B. Lotz, A. Marc, and K. Rahner, but it is not this group that dominates the numerous comments (*Zusätze*) which appear throughout the *Metaphysik*. Further, it is noteworthy that Coreth's own research has concentrated so heavily on Kant and Hegel.[23]

Consonant with and confirmative of all this is the marked difference between Maréchal's and Coreth's reading of the history of philosophy. Maréchal saw the metaphysics of knowledge of St. Thomas (especially as synthesized in the 84th and 86th Questions of the *Prima Pars* of the *Summa*) as the definitive solution to the metaphysical problems of the ancients as well as of the earlier medieval thinkers.[24] It is here that Maréchal locates the valid and final realistic metaphysics. The subsequent decline of metaphysics, as Maréchal saw it, was due to the disintegration of the Thomistic Synthesis.[25] It was gradually forgotten. For Coreth, however, the sound tradition begins with Plato, is developed by St. Augustine and further refined by St. Bonaventure.[26] This tradition was eclipsed precisely by the triumph, not the collapse, of the Aristotelianism advocated by St. Thomas.[27] In this view, Descartes is the beginning of a return to the Platonic-Augustinian tradition, a return which continues through Kant and the German idealists into Rahner and Coreth.[28]

Thus in Coreth Transcendental Thomism is becoming more aware of its inner nature as well as of its true natural ancestry. It is not a version of Thomism. It lines up rather with the *Via Platonica* which is incompatible with Thomistic metaphysical realism.[29]

According, then, to Coreth not only is the Transcendental Method the only valid method for metaphysics, not only is it the culmination of a long tradition that goes back—not to Aristotle but to Plato—but it is also the great contribution of Kant who explicitly identified, analyzed and used it. For Coreth the Transcendental Method, viewed in its purity, is an ahistorical permanent position, though it has been only imperfectly understood and defectively carried out by its great practitioners Kant, Fichte, Schelling, Hegel and, in a way, by Husserl and Heidegger.[30] Coreth's researches dealing with these philosophers was a guide to his understanding of the Transcendental Method and made it possible for him to separate it from the defects of its various concrete realizations. Muck notes, "Even this brief glance at some of the results of Coreth's investigation into the historical problems shows how a reflection on the failures of the Transcendental Method can yield *invaluable hints with regard to its proper use.*"[31] (Emphasis added).

Thus for Coreth, the corrected and purified Transcendental Method as he describes it in the *Metaphysik* (pages 55-94) is not a method tied to and conditioned by the history of modern philosophy but a permanently valuable method—*the* methodology of metaphysics. As such it should not be essentially tied to any dated presupposition or parochial problems.

In order to evaluate this apotheosis of the Transcendental Method into an idealized Platonic realm, we must review the origins of the Kantian *Critique*.

It is clear that at the end of the eighteenth century there

came a critical moment in the history of philosophy. Empiricism had come almost to its full logical term in Hume. Kant thought that if Hume could not be answered there would be an end not only to metaphysics but also to all scientific and rational knowledge. On the other hand the rationalism of Leibniz, Wolff, Baumgarten and of Kant himself appeared, after confrontation with Hume, to have no firm foundation. This philosophical confrontation was taking place in the period in which *the* great intellectual success was the new physics and the developing mathematics. In the same period, metaphysics appeared to be finally discredited. Kant tried to find a way out of this confrontation that would save, at least, the scientific rational knowledge of physics and mathematics. I repeat these well known facts because of two points.

First, it was quite understandable that Kant would accept as his presupposition or incorporate into his starting point that in which both traditions, that is, both parties to the confrontation, the Empiricists and the Rationalists, agreed, namely, that it is impossible to derive necessary and universal knowledge from experience and that, *a fortiori*, no transcendental could be in any way extracted therefrom.

Now it requires no subtle reworking to confront St. Thomas with this position. In the 84th Question of the *Prima Pars* of the *Summa*, he clearly and explicitly identified this position as one of the basic errors of the *Via Platonica* and firmly rejected it. It will be recalled that it was precisely in the 84th Question that Maréchal found the definitive establishment of metaphysical realism.[32]

Secondly, as Kant sought a methodological solution to his problem he did not even consider the sort of metaphysical realism that Maréchal, for example, identifies both as definitive philosophy and authentic Thomism. Gilson remarked, "I am well aware of the objections that

Kant might have made to the Aristotelian-Thomistic position, but, *as a matter of fact, he never gave it a thought.*"[33] (Emphasis added.)

There was good reason in eighteenth-century Germany for Kant to become the Kant of the *Critique.* There is no reason today to adopt a method, even in a modified form, that was a dated solution to a false problem.

But Coreth and Donceel are not merely adopting and modifying the Kantian methodology. They accept his presuppositions. Kant is credited with *seeing* that since all experienced objects were singular and contingent, no universality and necessity in knowledge could be derived from them. This alone excludes the experiential beginnings of Thomistic metaphysics and the intellective induction characteristic of Thomistic method.

But Coreth not only accepts Kant's presuppositions, when he inventories possible methods other than the Transcendental Method, he gives no more thought than did Kant to the type of method employed by St. Thomas.[34]

Now, we have seen that a methodology is intrinsically determined by its discipline and intrinsically determines the resulting discipline. To adopt a methodology that is not only different from but actually opposed to that of Thomism is to presuppose and to forecast—as Karl Rahner said—"an entirely new and different" system. There is no logical and consistent way in which the Transcendental Method can reconstruct the metaphysical realism of St. Thomas.

Let us examine this from another point of view. Maréchal, as we have seen, maintained that a sound Metaphysics of Being and of Knowledge exists—the Thomistic synthesis. He has also pointed out that the balanced solution to the philosophical antinomies developed by St. Thomas consists of a highly nuanced and unified body of theses.[35] Remove one of these theses and the whole collapses. There are no ad libitum positions in Thomism.[36] In fact, Maréchal develops his survey of post-Thomistic scholasticism in terms of the modification or rejection of the basic integrating theses.[37]

From what has already been said it is clear that Coreth alters theses basic to Thomism and, if Maréchal is right, thereby alters the whole synthesis. Throughout Coreth's *Metaphysik*, the repercussions are evident, though in this paper only a few instances can be examined.

At this point I think it is already clear, at least in a preliminary way, that one must choose between the Transcendental Method and the experiential realistic method of St. Thomas. One cannot have both. Transcendental Thomism is a contradiction in terms and in substance.

I will now examine a few illustrative instances from Coreth.

Coreth begins with questioning, the question which turns into the question of the question, and so turns on the conditions of the possibility of the question or of the *Vollzug*, the "performance," the "actuation" of the question.[38] The method does not ask about the "ontic" conditions—a condition whose *existence* is presupposed—or the logical conditions, which consist of the knowledge presupposed by the "content" of the question, but about the conditions of the "act" of the *Vollzug* and which therefore are co-affirmed in the act of questioning.[39] These are "transcendental" conditions. Thus the method begins with a *Vollzug* that is first found in precision from either an "ontic" subject of inherence or an "ontic" object to which the question is related.

Both Maréchal and Coreth insist that this is a "precision" and not, as in Kant, an "exclusion." But, from the standpoint of drawing a realistic metaphysics out of such a methodologically isolated starting point, there is no difference between a "precision" and an "exclusion." All the evidence of natural realism and all the evidence of the "critique of the object" said by Maréchal to be an essential thesis of Thomism (and this rightly, I believe) must be excluded from consideration as metaphysics develops. The rich evidence which Thomism initially uses must be derived from the *Vollzug* of the question. Thus, at page 177 an *Objekt-an-sich*, is reached for the first time—up to that point everything proceeds as though the questioner were alone; only at page 519 is the material world established and in pages 521-528 man's "sensibility" is deduced. When "matter" *is* reached, it turns out to be *Materialität* and quite differently conceived than the Thomistic *materia*. But now I revert to the establishment of the "other" as an *Objekt-an-sich*.[40]

Kant's use of the Transcendental Method brought him to a metaphysical agnosticism. Maréchal and Coreth both admit that in the succeeding phases of German Transcendentalism the efforts to break through the Kantian limitation to a new metaphysics have always terminated in an idealism. However, Maréchal and Coreth both maintain that the Transcendental Method can be corrected so as to overcome Kant and his followers and thereby avoid idealism.

This assertion is brought to the crucial test in pages 171-193 of the *Metaphysik*. Indeed, the transition from the subject to the object and the apodictic establishment of realism is said to be achieved at page 177: "*Hiermit entscheidet sich bereits*—vom Ansatz im Fragen her—das im neuzeitlichen Denken so zentrale Problem zwischen Idealismus und Realismus,—*Hiermit entscheidet sich bereits!*" At this point the debate between Idealism and Realism is settled![41]

The basis for this assertion is reduced back to the question about the conditions of possibility of questioning. When I ask a question, in the identity of the *Vollzug* of my question I know myself as the questioner and the other as the questioned. Thus the opposition of subject and object is set up within the *Vollzug* itself. But—I quote—"Es ist noch nicht ein Gegensatz, der an sich gesetzt und im Vollzug des Fragens und Wissens vorausgesetzt ist: noch nicht der Gegensatz von 'Subjekt-an-sich' und 'Objekt-an-sich!'"[42] It is important to pause here and reflect on this moment of the Transcendental Method. For the sake of argument, I pass over the problem of the *Subjekt-an-sich*. At this point the *Objekt im Vollzug, das Gefragte, das Gewusste* is simply an object held in thought, in the act of questioning.

Now, however, moving on, when I ask about "das" or "dieses," I already know something about the "das" or "dieses," otherwise I could not ask. But the "das" or "dieses" that I already know about is, from the standpoint of the Transcendental Method the *Objekt im Vollzug*. It is simply the logical (or Transcendental) subject of the question. It does not carry with it the ontic implications of ordinary common sense. "Es ist im Wissen gesetzt." Now, if I ask, I don't know all about it. I am asking for something *noch nicht im Wissen gesetzt*. But now, the argument runs, if I ask about "it" (the object of *Vollzug*), I don't know all about it. I am asking for something *noch nicht in Wissen gesetzt*. To keep this purely transcendental, I am asking what additional predicates can be added to the logical subject which I am holding in the *Vollzug*. These predicates are not yet contained in the *Vollzug*. But, says Coreth, it is a condition of the possibility of the *Vollzug* of the question that there be an Objekt-an-sich! Otherwise the question has no meaning. "...Wäre es nicht vorausgesetzt, so wäre die Möglichkeit des Fragens grundsätzlich aufgehoben." This transition from the *Gefragte*, as an object of thought, "Objectum im Vollzug," to an "Objekt-an-sich" that is not contained in the *Vollzug* nor presupposed as known in previous knowledge is, however much elaborated, the perennial illegitimate transition from thought to thing. If I, unthematically or however, know the specific *Objekt-an-sich* prior to the specific question, the question of realism would arise at that prior point and not within the subsequent questions. This would force a reductive consideration of initial natural realism which the Method has closed to Coreth.

The weight of the argument rests on the assumption that although the basis of the question is an object of thought which gives rise to the question, the question moves to an *Objekt-an-sich*, a reality independent of the subject and of the *Vollzug*. But it is far more consistent and logical to say that if I am asking a question about an object of thought, the answer should be in the same order—either another related object of thought (the *Gewusste* that is basic to the question) or an expansion of the given object of thought. After all, the development of Physics and Mathematics requires questioning and such development is quite consistent within the Kantian system. When I ask whether in a right triangle the square on the hypotenuse is equal to the sum of the squares on the other two sides I know something about a triangle; I don't know the answer to my question, but I don't have to postulate an *Objekt-an-sich*. I can work out the answer within the order of knowledge and so pass on to another *Vollzug*. The only way the argument will work is to assume a "das" which I already know to be an *Objekt-an-sich*. In reverting to a common sense analysis of asking a question, Coreth surreptitiously gives the argument a basis in natural realism which, theoretically, he should repudiate. The implicit realism must be washed out. Gilson, with profound insight, has noted that the idealistic systems can maintain themselves only by constantly, surreptitiously and, if you will, unthematically relying on natural realism. We must conclude that both the Transcendental Method and the methodic use of The Question fail at this critical point.

Coreth has not escaped the idealistic consequences of his method. From these ill-starred pages (171-193) to page 488 no additional argument is introduced to establish realism.

Another crucial test can be found in the argument given in pages 204-209.

First, I must call attention to the footnote on page 207. Three things are here asserted: 1) That the argument in the text is a proof for the existence of God (the first to be offered in the *Metaphysik*). 2) That no appeal is made to efficient causality. 3) That the basis of the argument is the "insight" ("*Einsicht*") that "every multiplicity presupposes a unity which makes that multiplicity possible." Now in the body of the text, the situation to which this insight (or "Principle") is applied is my knowledge of being as the identity in the difference of beings, that is, as a formal identity in real difference. If we pass over Coreth's previous failure to establish the existence of beings (*Seiende*) distinct—ontically—from the subject and from each other, the statement that there are really distinct individual beings may be assumed to be obvious. Now, however, we ask what is meant by a "formal identity" (*die formale Identität*)? It is distinguished from the real difference (*die reale Differenz*). If we take the word "form" to express that which makes a being to be what it is, there is no identity in the difference ("*in der Differenz*"), for the formal elements in the beings are as ontically or really different as the beings themselves. In our knowledge of individuals we can see that they are similar (not "identical") in some respect or other and so express this similarity in an abstract (materially) universal concept. The unification is not in the difference, not in beings, but in the intellect. Coreth moves to specify that the identity of all beings is being (*das Sein*). The movement of the argument goes then from the real difference through the formal identity to the existence of an absolute identity which must be absolute being (*absolutes*

Sein). Once it is recognized that the formal identity is an identity (or unification) in knowledge, the ontological progression of the argument is broken and we are dealing with a modern sophisticated version of Platonism (or, probably better, neo-Platonism). Coreth, in the attached *Zusatz*, expressly recognizes the Platonic background of the principle. In Plato he says, *"Die Gemeinsamkeit in der Verschiedenheit der Dinge verlangt als Grund der Einheit die transzendente Idee."* He properly relates this to the Kantian search for a principle of unity, that is, for the *"Einheit in der Mannigfaltigkeit."* St. Thomas himself identified this principle as Platonic. However, in imbedding it in his own argument he transforms it into a principle of efficient causality instead of a formality. This is in accord with his usual handling of "positiones" and enables him to pair it with an Aristotelian text. Coreth, however, expressly repudiates the use of efficient causality and is thus involved in the Platonic confusion of thought and thing, of formality and reality.

Now, I next select an illustrative case from Coreth's structuring of limited beings.

At page 213 Coreth undertakes to mediate (in the sense of "vermitteln") the metaphysical constitution of the individual beings. Now, even if the argument terminating on page 177, truly established an *Objekt-an-sich*, it told us nothing of the nature of that object, whether it was one or many, directly or indirectly known, or anything else about it. So now we must presuppose the existence of many, individual and limited entities (*Seiende*) which are different from me (after all, at this point even on Coreth's showing I know nothing of any other *Geist* except God) and from each other. Again, the substitution of questions about the individuals of our experience for the question about *das Sein im Ganzen* surreptitiously puts back into the method a large dose of natural realism. Knowledge of individuals is the condition for the possibility of questions about individuals. The questions about individuals are directed to determining what separates beings from each other and from *das Sein im Ganzen*.[53]

Essence (*Essentia; Wesen*) is discovered as the inner principle which limits being (*Sein*). It is found to be a "relative-negation" or a "negative-relation." This relationship to others is precisely what gives the limited beings their limitation and their determination. *Wesen* is neither being (*Sein*) nor an existent (*Seiendes*). In negative-relation to others, it denies the determination of others of its own existent, declares it "impossible." Thus it is seen as the potentiality of the determined limited being content of the existent. But its relative-negation and negative-relation to others underlies and is prior to its being itself a limited and determined possibility of being.[54] The difficulty here seems to be that Being (*Sein*) is not regarded as the act of existence and therefore the actuation of all acts but as a sort of Platonic universal—the *Sein alles Seienden*—which does not truly admit of an internal ontological (in Coreth's sense) analogy and is always in its full purity unlimited. The Platonic problem of non-being is thus resurrected and it is not surprising that a Platonizing solution is put forth—that essence should be seen as a relative-negation and a negative-relation which not only reproduces the Platonic principle of "otherness" but echoes the Spinozan establishment of the finite as a relative negation. One can say that what is positive in essence is here absorbed into Being as opposed to essence, and essence ceases to be a "real" component in the metaphysical order. Wilhelmsen, working along a somewhat different line of criticism, has uncovered this same fundamental weakness in Transcendental Thomism—the fundamental reduction of essence "to be *nothing more* (emphasis in the original) than a limit on existence..."[55]

After studying the discussion of essence (*Wesen*) in pages 217-249, one would expect to find the metaphysical (Coreth's "ontological") function of form to be likewise reduced to a minimum. And this is exactly what we find. Although essence (*Wesen*) is ontologically analyzed and established by page 249, "Form" is not discussed until pages 500-509. Form turns out to be simply a principle (ontological to be sure) which determines the material principle. Its function as act in its own order, of constituting the reality of the existent (of the *id quod est*) is almost completely (or perhaps completely) lost in Coreth's metaphysical (ontological) constitution of beings. The important role of form in the Thomistic metaphysical structure of finite beings almost totally disappears.

I have been able in this paper to give only a very preliminary and general assessment of Coreth's *Metaphysik* and of its relationship to the work of Maréchal. Much more extended analysis will be necessary to give a thoroughgoing critique. The project is rendered particularly difficult by a constant ambiguity of terminology. Thus we have seen that *Wesen*, though spoken of in Thomistic terminology, carries rather a Platonizing meaning.

This is particularly apparent in one absolutely basic theme which I shall only touch on here.

The Transcendental Thomists allege that the great fault in Kantianism is the total lack of or disregard for being. To turn the Transcendental Method into a Thomistic Transcendental Method and to turn the critical philosophy into a true metaphysics, "being" must be introduced as the central theme.

This is undoubtedly correct. But what understanding of being and what derivation of being?

Since the presuppositions of Kant have been accepted, neither the common not the metaphysical understanding of being can be derived or extracted from the objects of our direct experience. Donceel, writing in his own name, explains, "That is why metaphysics is *a priori*, virtually inborn in us, not derived from sense experience, exactly as the soul is ontologically prior to the body and not derived from it. Yet we would never know any metaphysics if we had no sense knowledge, exactly as our soul cannot operate without our body. Hence, metaphysics is *virtually* inborn in us. We become aware of it only *in* and *through* sense knowledge, although it does not come *from* sense knowledge."[56] This is, of course, the Kantian view that *a priori* knowledge arises with experience, on its occasion, but not from it.

Thus we never truly "learn" about being; we simply become aware of what we have known all along. There need be no experiential check on metaphysics nor do we have to go through the laborious development of our understanding of being which is the substance and the vitality of Thomistic Metaphysics. This understanding is given in advance—since it cannot be derived from experience—; it is already but "unthematically" known; it and its laws are "virtually" inborn. "The Question" presupposes it in an "absolute" and "self-identical" way. It is seen as *das Sein alles Seienden*. What does this mean?

Donceel, in his "Preface," adverts to the problem of translation created by the German language and Coreth's use of "being" terminology.[57] There is certainly a translation problem here, but, beyond that, there is an intrinsic difficulty of philosophical meaning. On page 141, in *Zusatz* 3 Coreth gives at least three different meanings for *Sein*.

Many other words occur. In discussing the Suarezian position *"Dasein"* is *"Existentia"* and *"Sosein"* is *"Quidditas,"* whereas the Thomistic *esse et essentia* becomes *Sein und Wesen*.[48]

While Coreth recognizes the Thomistic use of *esse* as the *actus essendi* which is distinct from the essence, the metaphysical emphasis does not fall here. In fact, while admitting the distinction, Coreth maintains that he has gone beyond it. What goes beyond it is precisely the negative-relation and the relative-negation of the essence, discussed above.[59]

Now, in Coreth the truly metaphysical expression is *das Sein alles Seienden*. I can see no way of translating this into Thomistic Latin. *Ens omnis entis* means nothing. The *Sein* here cannot be translated as *esse*, i.e., *actus essendi*. Coreth precisely denies this meaning. Moreover, to say that the *esse omnis entis* is that which binds all existents together would be sheer pantheism. The *Sein alles Seienden* is that which makes all beings to be beings (not "to exist"); and it is that in which all beings are united and that which is intrinsically common to all beings. There is only one tradition in which this makes sense—the Platonic tradition. The *Sein alles Seienden* must be translated as the Beingness of all beings and treated like a Platonic idea. We saw above that in the constitution of an existent all its being, all its positiveness, comes from the beingness that makes it a being. Since this pure beingness is "absolute," that is, completely purified and separated, it cannot be limited of itself—but by something outside itself. This brings us back to Coreth's problem of the essence as being outside the beingness of the existent. Analogous problems arise when Coreth deals with *"Materialität"* and "Forma." This Platonic turn explains also why Coreth believes his formalistic non-causal argument for the existence of God can work. Beingness is pure self-identity, pure unity; it is shared in by a diversity which violates its identity and yet without it would fall apart into pure multiplicity.

CONCLUSION
In this paper I have attempted to present, briefly and selectively, evidence in support of the following assertions

which express my current view.

1) The realistic metaphysical methodology of St. Thomas is different from and incompatible with any reasonably authentic version of the Transcendental Method.

2) That the use of the Transcendental Method results in an idealistic-oriented Platonizing metaphysics which is radically different from Thomistic metaphysics.

3) That Transcendental Thomism has no philosophical right to be called "Thomism."

4) That Transcendental Thomism is internally inconsistent and metaphysically unsound.

As an independent and final observation I should like to add that Maréchal's grand strategy for bringing Thomism into the mainstream of modern thought has obviously failed. I suggest that in this regard Jacques Maritain has been far more successful—and precisely because his was an authentic Thomism.

1. Cf. Otto Muck, S.J., *The Transcendental Method*, trans. William D. Seidensticker (New York: Herder & Herder, 1968), pp. 12-13. (Henceforth referred to as: Muck). Muck lists J. Maréchal, S.J., J. de Vries, S.J.,.A. Marc, S.J., G. Isaye, E. Coreth, K. Rahner, S.J., B.J.F. Lonergan, S.J., A. Gregoire, J.B. Lotz. We may add Joseph Donceel, S.J. and Gerald McCool, S.J.

2. Cf. Etienne Gilson, *The Unity of Philosophical Experience* (New York: Charles Scribner's Sons, 1947), p. 301:

   "On the other side, all those subtle shades of thoughts which qualify the principles of a philosopher, soften their rigidity and allow them to do justice to the complexity of concrete facts, are not only part and parcel of his own doctrine, but are often the only part of it that will survive the death of the system. We may wholly disagree with Hegel, or with Comte, but nobody can read their encyclopedias without finding there an inexhaustible source of partial truths and of acute observations. Each particular philosophy is, therefore, a co-ordination of self and mutually limiting principles which defines an individual outlook on the fullness of reality."

   What Gilson says here of all great philosophers applies to the Transcendental Thomists, especially since they retain many basic Thomistic insights.

3. "As he [Coreth] points out (p. 12) what has come from Fr. Maréchal is not a school but a movement, not a set of ready-made opinions repeated in unison by members of a uniform group, but a basic line of thought that already has

developed in various manners and still continues to do so." Bernard J.F. Lonergan, "Metaphysics as Horizon" in Emerich Coreth, *Metaphysics*, English edition by Joseph Donceel (New York: Herder & Herder, 1968), p. 200. (Henceforth this translation will be referred to as: Donceel).

4. Joseph Maréchal, *Le Point de départ de la métaphysique*, 3rd ed. (Paris: Desclée de Brouwer, 5 vols., vol. I, 1944; vol. II, 1949. Henceforth referred to as: Maréchal, I or II). See Muck, p. 26.

The 1949 edition of Cahier V was published after Maréchal's death, having been edited by L. Malevez, S.J. Maréchal had resisted efforts to republish the 1926 edition because he wished to revise, not his doctrine, but his presentation. Malevez made very few changes in the 1926 text, but he added (pp. 599-608) some comments originally published by Maréchal himself in the *Revue Néo-Scolastique de Philosophie*, 41 (1938): 253-261, as "A Propos du Point de Départ de la Métaphysique." See also: "Notes de Métaphysique," *Nouvelle Revue Théologique*, 53 (1926): 329-334, 447-451, 510-525; "Au seuil de la métaphysique: abstraction ou intuition," *Revue Néo-Scolastique de Philosophie*, 31 (1929): 27-52, 121-147, 309-342 (reprinted in *Mélanges Joseph Maréchal*, Vol. 1 [Bruxelles-Paris, 1950, pp. 288-298]. "Les premiers écrits philosophiques du P. Maréchal," *Mélanges*, Vol. I, pp. 23-46. "Jugement 'scolastique' concernant la racine de l'agnosticisme kantien," first written in 1914 but first published in *Mélanges*, Vol. I, pp. 273-287. "Le dynamisme intellectuel dans la connaissance objective," *Revue Néo-Scolastique de Philosophie*, 28 (1927), pp. 137-165 (Reprinted in *Mélanges*, Vol. I, pp. 75-101); "Phénoménologie pure ou philosophie de l'action," *Philosophie Perennis* (Regensburg, 1930), Vol. I, pp. 377-400 (Reprinted in *Mélanges*, Vol. I, pp. 181-206). "Le problème de dieu' d'après M. Edouard L. Roy," *Nouvelle Revue Théologique*, 58 (1931): 193-216, 289-316 (Reprinted in *Mélanges*, Vol. I, pp. 107-259). "L'aspect dynamique de la méthode transcendentale chez Kant," *Revue Néo-Scolastique de Philosophie*, 43 (1959): 341-384.

5. "Das neue transzendental-metaphysische Denken hat sicher schon bedeutende Leistungen vollbracht, aber es hat seine Aufgabe noch lange nicht erfüllt. Diese Aufgabe heisst, die gesamte Metaphysik von Grund auf neu zu durchdenken, d. h. von einem ersten Ansatz her methodisch zu begründen und systematisch zu entwickeln. Dies soll hier im Grundriss versucht werden. Dazu ist vor allem eine differenziertere Fortbestimmung der transzendentalen Methode als der Grundmethode der Metaphysik erfordert. So wird auch in der Durchführung besonderes Gewicht gelegt auf die kritisch-methodische Selbstbegründung der Metaphysik, die in den ersten Abschnitten vollzogen wird." Emerich Coreth, *Metaphysik* (Innsbruck: Tyrolia, 1961), p. 13. (Henceforth this work will be referred to as: Coreth).

6. Maréchal, V: 66-71.

7. Lonergan's only published comment that deals directly with Coreth is his review of the *Metaphysik*, originally published as a review article in the *Gregorianum*, 44 (1963): 307-318 and reprinted at the end of Donceel's English version of the *Metaphysik*, pp. 197-219. This review adds little to the under-

standing of Coreth and it is, in fact, a rather superficial attack on the Thomistic realism of Gilson. In my opinion this is perhaps the weakest piece of philosophical writing ever produced by Fr. Lonergan. For example, the one thing Gilson has consistently rejected is that there is an epistemological problem of the "bridge." "Prof. Gilson acknowledges a problem of a bridge and so arrives at his need for an intellectual perception of being" (Donceel, p. 215). This is simply absurd. Professor Gilson finds that as a matter of fact we do grasp being in every perceptual judgment and, consequently, there is no problem of the "bridge." Moreover, Lonergan calls Coreth an "immediate realist" (Donceel, p. 210). This is so far from the truth that Coreth never reaches external reality. And why did Lonergan give no reference for this in an article full of page references?

8. Cf. Muck, pp. 276-277 and 284. Muck displays the uniqueness of Lonergan's position and his difference from Maréchal while claiming to find the transcendental method in Lonergan's work. "But we have been able to show that despite his *unique viewpoint and terminological peculiarities* (which are, of course, direct consequents of the *development of his viewpoint*), the *essential elements of transcendental analysis* can easily be discerned while the distinctness of his concrete expression demonstrates anew the extent of the development power of this method" (Muck, p. 284). (Emphasis added).

"By reason of its unrelenting insistence on the empirical, Lonergan's transcendental method should be carefully distinguished (despite other common themes) from various other transcendental analyses with which it is usually associated, e.g., those of J. Maréchal, K. Rahner, E. Coreth, and A. Marc in Otto Muck, *The Transcendental Method* (New York: Herder and Herder, 1968). Lonergan's attention to this topic dates from a series of historical articles originally published in the late 1940's and later republished together in one volume edited by David Burrell, *Verbum: Word and Idea in Aquinas* (Notre Dame: Univ. of Notre Dame Press, 1967)." Walter E. Conn, "Transcendental Analysis of Conscious Subjectivity," *The Modern Schoolman*, 3 (1977): 216.

9. "The philosophical events which have been described in the previous chapters cannot be wholly understood in the sole light of biography, of literary history, or even of the history of the systems in which they can be observed. They point rather to the fact that, in each instance of philosophical thinking, both the philosopher and his particular doctrine are ruled from above by an impersonal necessity. In the first place, philosophers are free to lay down their own sets of principles, but once this is done, they no longer think as they wish—they think as they can. In the second place, it seems to result from the facts under discussion, that any attempt on the part of a philosopher to shun the consequences of his own position is doomed to failure. What he himself declines to say will be said by his disciples, if he has any; if he has none, it may remain eternally unsaid, but it is there, and anybody going back to the same principles, be it several centuries later, will have to face the same conclusions. It seems, therefore, that though philosophical ideas can never be found separate from philosophers and their philosophies, they are, to some extent,

independent of philosophers as well as of their philosophies. Philosophy consists in the concepts of philosophers, taken in the naked, impersonal necessity of both their contents and their relations." E. Gilson, *The Unity of Philosophical Experience*, pp. 301-302.

10. In this view, Coreth is fulfilling the predictions made by Gilson in his criticism of the effort to combine, in any serious fashion, critical philosophy with Thomistic metaphysics. See E. Gilson, *Réalisme Thomiste et critique de la connaissance* (Paris: Vrin, 1939), pp. 130-212.

11. This is emphasized by the very title of Muck's book, "The Transcendental Method." "The question concerning methodology is an indication of a crisis," (Muck, p. 11). It is the method, the transcendental "stance" (Muck, p. 20), the transcendental "approach" (Muck, p. 21), the transcendental "turn" (Muck, p. 9). It is the use of this method that is the form of unity in the "movement" and the determining characteristic of Transcendental Thomism (Muck, p. 21).

12. "Vers la fin du Cahier (Livre III), nous userons de la seconde tactique indiquée plus haut, c'est-à-dire que nous rechercherons si les postulats initiaux du Kantisme (*objet phénoménal* et *méthode transcendentale d'analyse*) ne recéleraient pas, quoi qu'en ait cru Kant, l'affirmation implicite d'un véritable *objet* métaphysique. Qu'il faille répondre à cette question par un oui ou par un non, la valeur du réalisme ancien n'en demeure pas moins établie à nos yeux; nous ne jugeons pas toutefois ce surplus d'enquête totalement oiseux; car il y aurait bien quelque intérêt à constater que le réalisme métaphysique compénètre à tel point la pensée humaine qu'il est enveloppé déjà, de nécessité logique, dans la simple représentation "objective" d'une donnée quelconque." Maréchal, V: 15.

"La Critique ancienne se confond avec la systématisation métaphysique et ne s'achève qu'avec elle: c'est la *voie longue* de la critique; mais c'en est aussi, selon nous, le *procédé naturel*." Maréchal V: 60.

"La place reste libre pour une philosophie qui posséderait les avantages de l'Idéalisme transcendantal, sans en partager les tares essentielles: pour un finalisme rationnel, non rationaliste; pour une épistémologie qui réduise les prétentions illusoires de la raison, mais maintienne effective la suprématie de cette dernière sur l'entendement abstractif. "L'aristotélisme, précisé et complété—corrigé, si l'on veut—par les Scolastiques et plus particulièrement par S. Thomas, répond aux conditions ici posées." Maréchal V: 39.

13. Maréchal V: 66-71.

14. "S'il est vrai—c'est notre thèse dans ce volume—que la *Critique ontologique et la Critique transcendantale*, quoique différentes par le point de vue sous lequel elles envisage d'abord l'objet connu, convergent de droit vers un même résultat final traite l'une comme une simple transposition de l'autre." Maréchal I:70.

"Ces deux méthodes critiques, abordant, sous des angles complémentaires, le même objet total, doivent, poussées à fond, livrer finalement des conclusions identiques; car la Critique ancienne pose d'emblée l'Objet ontologique, qui inclut le Sujet transcendantal; et la Critique moderne s'attache au Sujet transcendantal, qui *postule* l'Objet ontologique." Maréchal V:60.

15. Donceel, pp. 7-14; Donceel, pp. 17-31; Coreth, p. 88; Coreth, p. 93.

16. Coreth, pp. 92-93.

17. Coreth, p. 55; Coreth, p. 94.

18. Coreth, p. 94.

19. R.J. Henle, S.J. *Saint Thomas and Platonism* (The Hague: Nijhoff, 1956), pp. 294-308.

20. Muck, pp. 9-10.

21. *Ibid*.

22. Coreth, pp. 12-13.

23. Muck, p. 286.

24. "Pour la première fois, l'antinomie de l'Un et du Multiple se trouve nettement et complètement résolue. Loin de sacrifier l'unité, comme Héraclite; ou la multiplicité, comme Parménide; loin de creuser un fossé, comme Platon, entre le sensible et l'intelligible; loin même de laisser, comme Aristote, la transcendance de l'unité absolue enveloppée encore d'incertitudes, Saint Thomas équilibre, d'une main sûre, ces éléments divers, dont il découvre, en tout acte de connaissance objective, le centre humain de perspective et d'ailleurs la synthèse vivante." Maréchal I: 121.

25. "Nous allons devoir montrer, au cours de longs chapitres, que la pensée philosophique, dès qu'elle abandonne ce point de vue central et privilégié, retombe dans des antinomies et rend enévitable l'essai d'une nouvelle critique de la connaissance." Maréchal I: 121.

26. Coreth, pp. 70-71.

27. Coreth, p. 70.

28. The Platonic affinities of Kantianism are not often recognized. Bergson detected them clearly: "Briefly, the whole *Critique of Pure Reason* ends *in establishing* that Platonism, illegitimate if Ideas are *things*, becomes *legitimate if Ideas are relations*, and that the ready-made idea, once brought down in this way from heaven to earth, is in fact, as Plato held, *the common basis alike of thought and of nature*. But the whole of the *Critique of Pure Reason* also rests on this postulate, *that our intellect is incapable of anything but Platonizing*—that is, of pouring all possible experience *into pre-existing moulds*." *Introduction to Metaphysics*, trans. T.E. Hulme (Indianapolis: Bobbs-Merrill, 1949), pp. 58-59.

29. See R.J. Henle, S.J., op. cit., pp. 322-350.

30. Coreth, pp. 35-43.

31. Muck, p. 288.

32. Maréchal I: 101-121. In these pages Maréchal repeatedly states that St. Thomas' solution is definitive.

33. Etienne Gilson, *Réalisme Thomiste et critique de la connaissance* (Paris: Vrin, 1939), pp. 167-168.

34. Coreth, pp. 88-93.

35. "Seuls les très grands systèmes philosophiques peuvent s'offrir à une épreuve éliminatoire aussi largement conçue: car elle s'étend à tous les plans de la réalité physique, psychologique, morale et religieuse. C'est précisément un des caractères les plus remarquables de la "synthèse thomiste" que d'avoir atteint cette universalité strictement enchaînée." Maréchal I:107.

36. "Dans le vrai thomisme, il ne resterait de thèses 'ad libitum,' interchangeables, que celles qui impliqueraient des problèmes fictifs, ou mal posés, ou insuffisamment mûris." *Ibid.*

37. Maréchal I: 217-222.

38. The problem of the "starting point" of metaphysics is of primary importance. As the old adage has it—a small error in the beginning becomes finally enormous—*parvus error in principio magnus fit in fine*. A distinction must be made. A personal approach to metaphysics may be made from almost any fact, a spark of a Roman candle, a love affair, a moral problem, a vague wonder about the meaning of things. But if one is thinking about the systematic starting point of a discipline already established, then there can be only one legitimate starting point. Since the starting point of metaphysics must be co-terminous with the human grasp of reality, it cannot possibly be the "question." I do not deal in this paper with this problem since I think that Professor Frederick Wilhelmsen has definitively shown that the "question" cannot possibly be the starting point of a metaphysics—certainly not of a realistic metaphysics. (See Frederick D. Wilhelmsen, "The Priority of Judgment over Question," *International Philosophical Quarterly*, 14, 4 (1974). While most of the other Transcendental Thomists started with an affirmation, a judgment, Karl Rahner defined the starting point of metaphysics as "questioning." *Spirit in the World*, trans. William Dych, S.J. (New York: Herder and Herder, 1968), pp. 57-65.

39. Coreth, pp. 104-109.

40. Coreth, pp. 176-180.

41. Coreth, p. 174.

42. Coreth, p. 174.

43. Coreth, p. 176.

44. Coreth, p. 176.

45. Coreth, pp. 176-177.

46. Coreth, p. 177.

47. *Ibid.* cf. Gilson, *Réalisme Thomiste et critique de la connaissance*, pp. 173-174.

48. Coreth, p. 204. Donceel also uses this argument in his own *Philosophical Psychology*, 2nd ed. (New York: Sheed and Ward, 1961), pp. 260-261.

49. Coreth, pp. 204-205.

50. Coreth, p. 209.

51. "Respondeo dicendum, quod omnis cognitio est per assimilationem; simili-

tudo autem inter aliqua duo est secundum convenientiam in forma. Cum autem unitas effectus unitatem causae demonstret, et sic in genere cujuslibet formae ad unum primum principium illius formae redire oporteat, impossibile est aliqua duo ad invicem esse similia, nisi altero duorum modorum: vel ita quod unum sit causa alterius, vel ita quod ambo ab una causa causentur, quae eamdem formam utrique imprimat;..." St. Thomas Aquinas, *De veritate*, I, 8, ad 8.

52. *S.T.* I, q. 44, a. 1, c.

53. Coreth, pp. 215-216.

54. Coreth, pp. 234-241.

55. Wilhelmsen, *op. cit.*, p. 493. cf. St. Thomas: "Essentia dicitur secundum quod per eam et in ea res habet esse." *De ente et essentia*, c. 1.

56. Donceel, p. 8.

57. Donceel, pp. 13-14.

58. Coreth, pp. 225-226.

59. Coreth, p. 243.

Looking At
The Future

Can St. Thomas Speak To The Modern World?

Leo Sweeney, S.J.

Loyola University, Chicago

The topic assigned me in this Symposium as to whether Thomas Aquinas can speak to the modern world is not easy. The difficulty is not so much determining whether Aquinas should be taken as a theologian or philosopher, although a controversy does exist as to whether and in what sense his writings are philosophical, a question which comes down to this: how can we in the twentieth century be helped philosophically by reading his *Summa Theologiae* and other theological treatises? An answer comes from accurately understanding how Aquinas conceives of "theology" and "philosophy," especially "Christian philosophy."

Secondly, the problem with my topic is not whether Aquinas *does* speak to the modern world: rather obviously, he does not—at least not often enough and with sufficient clarity to most of our contemporaries, for otherwise we would not be here at this session. The question rather is whether he *can* speak to the modern world. That is, does he still have anything genuinely significant and helpful to say in the twentieth century? Are his doctrines, as well as the insights from which they issue, really relevant to people today? Do they confront and help dissipate at least some problems on the contemporary scene? Are they influential on the modern mind?

For still another difficulty—and perhaps the most troublesome of all—which our topic entails, let us reflect on the words just used: "the modern world," "the twentieth century," "people today," "the contemporary scene," "the modern mind." What do those expressions mean? Are the "moderns" current professional philosophers only? Or also *hoi polloi*? In the USA? In the West only? In the East?

This paper will consist of three parts, the first two of which will concentrate on what the "modern mind" referred to from 1925 to 1960 and, secondly, from 1960 to the present time. The final portion of the paper will chart four areas in which Aquinas' doctrines seem especially relevant and helpful to our contemporaries.

A couple of comments before beginning with the paper itself. Greater attention to the "modern mind" seems called for than to Thomas Aquinas himself, since those attending this Symposium are already aware of his doctrines, which moreover subsequent papers will deal with—e.g.,Christian philosophy, transcendental Thomism, Gilson's and Maritain's interpretations of Aquinas, Thomas' ethics and metaphysics. Hence, our greater concentration on what "the modern mind" consists in seems justified.

Secondly, in describing the "makers" of the "modern mind," I may seem to be unduly negative by concentrating on their inadequacies. This concentration issues from my wishing to show how Aquinas can complement them and can remedy their inadequacies—hence, my wishing to show how Kant or Hegel or Freud may have erred appears necessary. This discussion should blind no one to the fact that each of them is an intellectual giant and that we profit from reading them. For example, how could we have appreciated the subject as subject or freedom if there had been no Descartes, no Kant, no Sartre?

This having been said, let us begin Part One of the paper: the "modern mind" from 1925 to 1960.

"THE MODERN MIND": 1925-1960

Consider, for instance, the last in the list: "the modern mind." In the mid-twenties Jacques Maritain investigated the "'roots and primal germinal forces' of the ideas which dominate our contemporary mind"[1] and found them to have come from three reformers: Luther, who reformed religion, Descartes philosophy, and Rousseau morality.[2] Their influence culminated (to quote from Gerald B. Phelan's article, "St. Thomas and the Modern Mind," which begins with references to Maritain's *Three Reformers*) in the philosophy of Immanuel Kant, who

> 'stands at the meeting of the intellectual streams springing from these three men.' From Descartes he inherited the conception of the independence of reason with respect to things; from Rousseau he inherited the conception of the independence of morality with respect to reason; from Luther he inherited the conception of the independence of religion with respect to authority. These ideas became the nucleus of the Kantian doctrine of transcendentalism in the realm of reason, autonomy in the realm of will and immanence in the realm of religion.[3]

From that moment on (Phelan continues) "Kant became the Pedagogue of Europe, the Maker of the Modern Mind." For with few exceptions (Phelan now turns to Cardinal Mercier's 1919 essay, "Le problème de la conscience moderne"), "the men who originated European thought for the last century and a half are permeated with the spirit of Kant."[4] That spirit of the *Critique of Pure Reason* it is (Phelan continues on his own) "which gave rise, though in different manners and with different results, to modern movements of thought as divergent as the idealism of Hegel, the materialism of Marx, the positivism of Comte, the intuitionism of

Bergson, and the pragmatism of William James."[5]

Phelan's 1942 article, together with the attention it gave to Maritain's earlier study, is interesting and useful, of course, by outlining the cure Aquinas offers to "the confusion [in philosophy, in morality, in religion] of the Modern Mind," which has resulted from the influence of Immanuel Kant, whose philosophy (we shall recall) both Maritain and Phelan considered to have itself resulted from the influence Luther, Descartes and Rousseau exerted on him. And what is that cure? Aquinas makes "order out of chaos in the world of thought" in these steps (p. 40). He firmly grounded "metaphysics on the solid rock of natural reason, i.e., the native capacity of man to know what is *in rerum natura*" (pp. 40-41), to know actual beings themselves, to know noumena. He then established metaphysics as the science of those noumenal beings precisely *as being*, as actually existing and, next, he stressed that "intelligibility is rooted in being and that knowledge follows, not conditions, being. Thence onward it was a question of ordering all thought in conformity with the order of being" (pp. 41-42). This Aquinas did by distinguishing the "four orders of being in relation to knowledge—the order of things known by the intellect but not made nor ordered by it, the order made by the intellect in its own concepts, the order made by the intellect in the acts of the will and the order made by the intellect in external works (the speculative, the logical, the moral and the artistic orders, respectively)—and the whole plan of the structure of philosophical wisdom was clear" (p.42).

But interesting and useful as Phelan's paper is for its outline of Aquinas' cure for the confused modern mind, it holds another and possibly greater value for us: it helps illumine what the "modern mind" is which Aquinas will possibly aid. According to Maritain and Phelan (to paraphrase the New Testament),

Luther, Descartes and Rousseau begot Kant; Kant begot Hegel, Marx, Comte, Bergson and James; Hegel begot Hitler and Mussolini, Marx begot Lenin, Stalin and Mao [for the moment let us attend only to Hegel and Marx]; Hitler and Mussolini begot the Nazis of the Third Reich and the Italian Fascists; Lenin, Stalin and Mao begot the Communists in Russia and Eastern Europe, in China and North Korea.

That family record discloses several facets of the "modern mind." A few thinkers in Europe (Luther, Descartes, Rousseau, Kant, Hegel, Marx) and the books they authored influenced billions of people throughout the world. Secondly, what began in speculation ended in practice. What started with abstract ideas soon descended inevitably to the concrete, daily lives of individual women, men and their children.

These aspects of the "modern mind" reveal the importance and difficulty of our topic, which is not merely speculative, academic, esoteric, abstract, impersonal, impractical. No, it has repercussions which are intensely practical, concrete, personal and affecting the everyday lives of billions of people. Paul Dezza, S.J., said on October 14, 1941, in a conference given in Rome, "Scholastic Philosophy Faces Modern Thought," (p. 12): "Ideas direct the world and are at the foundation of all social upheavals." Let me illustrate with Etienne Gilson's remarks on Hegel in *The Unity of Philosophical Experience* (1937).[6]

'The truth is the whole,' and the whole itself is nature, which reaches 'its completeness through the process of its own development.' ...Nature is but the external manifestation of an absolute and eternal Idea [*Geist*], which expresses itself in space and time according to a dialectical law...The Idea which thus 'alienates' itself in nature is finding its way back through the successive moments of

its dialectical realization. Each term of a concrete anti-
nomy thus becomes a necessary step to the final self-
reassertion of the Idea. That was a master stroke, but it
entailed the open recognition of the fact that contradiction was at the very root of reality...Intelligible as part of
the whole, each particular thing is unintelligible by itself;
rather, by itself, it is but a self-affirmation grounded on
the negation of the rest, and denied by the rest. If the
realization of the Idea is the march of God through the
world, the path of the Hegelian God is strewn with ruins.

In a metaphysical system wherein the whole of reality
is included, such a doctrine does not limit itself to ideas, it
applies to things [and men]...That which is contradiction
between ideas is war between men, and in such a world
war is by no means an accident. It is law. The progressive
actualization of the world-leading Idea entails the sub-
mission of individuals to the unity of the State. The ideal
State itself is progressively working out its unity through
the necessary oppositions between particular states.

Indeed, Hegel teaches that "taken by itself, no particular
thing can rightly assert itself except by destroying another,
and until it is itself destroyed. 'War,' says Hegel, 'is not an
accident,' but an element 'whereby the ideal character of the
particular receives its right and reality.' These are really and
truly murderous ideas, and all the blood for which they are
responsible has not yet been shed."

How prophetic Gilson's words were can be gathered
from the fact that he spoke them in lectures delivered at
Harvard during the Fall semester of the 1936-1937 academic
year.[7]

You will, I hope, pardon such a long quotation from
Gilson, but he, together with Maritain and Phelan, aids us
in understanding what "the modern mind" meant in the

decades between 1930 and (say) 1960. It referred to all human individuals during those years as they lived out their day-by-day existence in socialist and fascist nations; also, all human individuals during those years in countries threatened and, then, at war with those nations. And if we now bring in Auguste Comte, Henri Bergson and William James, "the modern mind" deals with absolutely every human person affected by atheism and capitalism (to the extent these are influenced by Comte's positivism), by relativism in ethics (to the extent influenced by Bergson's conviction that reality *is* change); by utilitarian and pragmatic conceptions of truth and conduct (to the extent influenced by William James). "The modern mind" expresses, then, an enormous number of human persons—all those affected in their concrete and practical lives by the "makers" of the modern mind Maritain and Phelan listed. And the title of Phelan's paper on "St. Thomas and the Modern Mind" was equivalent to his asking whether Aquinas can speak to the modern mind, an inquiry which we heard him answering affirmatively—not that he expected all (or even many) individual members of that vast multitude themselves to catch and/or accept Aquinas' messages; but that he thought some of Aquinas' positions on reality, God, knowledge, the human person, morality are so valid, true and relevant as to merit the thirteenth-century Dominican a place with the other "makers of the modern mind" (maybe even displace some of them?) if only his doctrines were authentically set forth in the classrooms of all schools, Catholic and non-Catholic, throughout the world; if only, too, they were widely communicated through the printed page and through other media so that they became an essential ingredient of cultures everywhere and thus operative in the everyday thinking and decisions and living of everyone.

As the preceding remarks suggest, then, the phrase, "the modern mind," involves several factors: (1) a thinker whose writings or lectures contain (2) ideas which are pivotal, germinal, dynamic, energizing and (3) which come to be disseminated so widely (4) that they infiltrate and deeply affect the majority of people in an era and a place (5) in what they think and say, in how they act and react. These latter (the majority of individuals) are directly the "modern minds"; the former (the man or woman of ideas) is the "maker" of modern minds; in between are the disseminators, propagandizers and popularizers, who are "makers" too in an important but subordinated and derived sense.

All of them were, for Phelan, Maritain and Gilson, the "modern minds" whom Thomas could have benefited. Thus, he could have become a "maker" of the modern mind, especially given the facts that Maritain and Gilson had unearthed a much more authentic Thomism that had been almost totally hidden since the death of Aquinas himself, that Thomism was widely taught on Catholic campuses and with considerable success,[8] that through their writings and through their lectures at Princeton, Harvard, Yale and elsewhere Maritain and Gilson had an audience too in non-Catholic circles. But one need only recall World War II, its aftermath in the '50s, our own two decades of the '60s and '70s to realize that their efforts and ours were not completely successful.

"THE MODERN MIND": 1960 TO THE PRESENT

The mention of the sixties and seventies reopens our original question: can St. Thomas speak to the modern minds of our decades? Who are they? Of course, some of our contemporaries (in fact, more now than ever before) still live under totalitarian regimes (Russia, Poland, Lithuania and other countries of Eastern Europe, as well as Cuba, some areas in Africa and Latin America; China, North Korea, Vietnam).[9] The "makers" of their minds are, not surprisingly, the same as for people living under communism in earlier decades: Lenin, Stalin and Mao, whose fathers (so to speak) are Hegel and Marx and whose grandfather is Kant. Other contemporaries are capitalists (still due remotely to Comte?), ethical situationalists (due remotely to Bergson?), pragmatists and utilitarians (William James' influence?).

Are there other groups in the West? In his syndicated column of March 13, 1979, George F. Will stated that "the three makers of the modern mind and of the modern sense of disorder today are Darwin, Freud, Einstein."[10] Why so? His answers, the first of which comes at the beginning of his column and the second at its end, are elliptic but provocative.

> The essence of modern consciousness, which Einstein did so much to shape, is that things are not what they seem. Charles Darwin asserted a continuum between man and lesser matter. Sigmund Freud's theme, developed in his work on infant sexuality, is that there are uncharted continents of mysterious depths within us. According to modern physics, a person pounding a table is pounding mostly space and electricity—and the person doing the pounding is mostly space and electricity [too].... Matter, Einstein said, is [simply] a form of energy. To increase the speed of an object is to contract the passage of its time. Light is pulled down by gravity because light is subject, at some point, to laws governing substantial objects. And last month scientists announced evidence of gravity waves—evidence that further confirms Einstein's vision: gravitic energy is a form of radiation. Things are not what they seem.

In the final paragraphs the columnist turns again to Darwin, Freud and the physicist.

Copernicus removed mankind from the center of the universe, but at least Newton said the universe is intelligible, even decorous. Newton was a great orderer, whose clockwork theory of the universe gave rise, through the seepage of science into the wider culture, to clockwork art—the dignified classicism of the 18th century. And it gave rise to clockwork political theory, the clearest expression of which is the U.S. Constitution, a serene system of "checks and balances."...

Then came the three makers of the modern mind and of the modern sense of disorder—Darwin, Freud, Einstein. Darwin imbedded man in the mud, or, more precisely, he said mankind is continuous with the slime from which mankind has crept. Rather than nature's final word, mankind may be an early bead on an endless string.

Darwin gave an unsentimental view of the childhood of the species [but] Freud gave an unsentimental view of childhood. And he linked the artifices of civilization with the uncaged furies in the jungle within man.

Newtonian physics could be explained visually, at least a bit, for laymen, on a billiard table. But Einsteinian physics wraps in uncertainty the concepts we use, from childhood on, to make sense of everyday experience— the concepts of space, time, matter. Modern physics puts laymen severely in their place, which is outside the conversation of science. Yet Einstein, who expanded our sense of life's mysteriousness, insisted that the essential Einsteinian insight is philosophic...and it is this: the difference between what the most and the least learned people know is inexpressibly trivial in relation to all that is unknown.

Why does Will consider that famous biologist, psychologist and physicist to have produced the contemporary mind? For two reasons, the first of which is that each of them has caused us to believe that things are not what they seem. However much a man may appear to have immaterial dimensions and powers, he is material since matter is a continuum of which he is a part (Darwin). However normal and well adjusted someone may seem, he contains deep, dark, mysterious forces conditioning or, even threatening his psychological equilibrium constantly (Freud). However solid and matter-of-fact physical objects (including men) may seem, they are mostly space and electrical charges, the matter of which they are made is itself a form of energy, speed is translated into time, gravity into radiation (Einstein). And these beliefs in a thing's not being what it appears result in our conviction (often subconscious but effective) that our spontaneous knowledge must yield to technical knowledge if we are to escape deception: spontaneous knowledge left uncorrected deceives us as to the true nature of reality. And we can be left feeling uneasy, uncertain, wary, depressed, vaguely guilty.

The second reason why Darwin, Freud and Einstein are "makers" of contemporary mentality is that each makes us realize that a human existent does not amount to much— certainly, his cognitive powers and spiritual dimension (if this latter exists at all) are minimal and not worthy of much praise. Each of us has crept from slime and, figuratively, is merely one "early bead on an endless string" (Darwin). Each carries within himself a jungle of uncaged Furies (Freud). No one can make sense of his own everyday spatial, temporal, material universe without assistance from trained scientists, and the intellectual ability and accomplishments of even the best of these are totally trivial in the face of what still remains unknown (Einstein). And, again, feelings of inadequacy, unworthiness, frustration, fright can befall us, thereby experiencing "the modern sense of disorder" which the columnist traces to those three "makers" of the contemporary mind. An inference to be drawn from his account of them is that a human individual is, in the last analysis, of little value and significance.

In stark and explicit contrast to this view is existentialism, according to which each human person alone is real. Worthwhileness and significance—in a word, reality—resides in the uniqueness, never-to-be-repeatedness, originality of a human individual who is "actually exercising his freedom. The reason why he is unique and uniquely so is that he is *free*. He is a human existent, endowed with intellect and will, who thus can freely fashion himself and stand-out from others. This uniqueness is not in the abstract or in the past or even in the future: it is in the concrete, here-and-now exercise of his freedom in this or that choice, which is his and no other's and which even he himself can never reduplicate exactly, because any other decision will be at least numerically distinct and because he will never again find himself in these identical circumstances."[11]

Such is the basic reaction of all radical existentialists, whether atheist or theist, to the downgrading of individual men and women by biology, psychoanalysis or physics. And Sartre, Camus, Heidegger, Marcel, Buber and the rest all take their initial cue from Kierkegaard. "The evolution of the whole world," he wrote in 1847, "tends to show the absolute importance of the category of the individual apart from the crowd." In 1848: "Each human being has infinite reality." In 1850: "In the eyes of God, the infinite spirit, all the millions that have lived and now live do not make a crowd: He only sees each individual."[12]

Fathered by Kierkegaard, those existentialists have themselves begotten groups in the anti-war years of the 1960s with such interesting names as the "New Breed," the "Free Speech Movement," "Hippies," the "Woodstock Generation," with its hard rock and hard drugs, the "Flower Children;" the "Me-generation" in the current protests against nuclear energy; in more peaceful circumstances the nameless aspirants to a simple life-style where love and tolerance should reign; the charismatics. But however diverse in name and style, all of them have in common the conviction that each individual human existent is supremely and solely important and, therefore, real. And this conviction issues into two norms for practical life. Each person is to determine *for himself* what he shall do and what his values are.[13] Secondly, let us all love one another, since each individual is worthwhile and, therefore, lovable—"Make love, not war," so the slogan goes.

AQUINAS A "MAKER" OF CONTEMPORARY MINDS?

Existentialists, then, are among our contemporaries and their presence should allow us to answer the question of this paper somewhat more easily. Can Thomas speak to our contemporaries? Are his doctrines relevant today? Do they help dissipate current problems? Will our contemporaries listen to him? The fact that Thomas also is an existentialist, rightly and authentically understood, should win him, initially at least, an audience, and the fact that his is an authentic existentialism could alert them to the possibility of a genuine humanism which gives a primacy to man but not at the expense of what is nonhuman (e.g., God). Let me explain briefly.

Existentialism is a philosophical position in which primacy is given to "existence" (whatever that noun may mean), in which "existence" confers reality because it bestows perfection, worthwhileness, significance upon whatever *is* perfect, worthwhile, significant. In short, it is a doctrine where "to be real" is "to exist." But what is "existence"? For Sartre, Marcel, Heidegger and so on, "to exist" is "to be human." Only men, only subjects are real in the sense of intrinsically and *per se* being perfect, valuable, significant, and what makes them alone be real is the fact that they *are subjects* actually exercising their freedom (see paragraph above corresponding to note 11). Such a philosophical position is an existentialism (although unauthentic because "existence" here does not mean—at least in English—what it seems to mean by force of the term itself) and it is an absolute (or exaggerated) humanism because only man is real and everything nonhuman (God and subhumans) are not real in themselves but solely if and as men project or use them.

But "to exist" can also be taken as "to be actual" and then any actual existent, no matter what sort it may be, is real by the very fact that it actually exists. Reality is not restricted to any one kind of being, whether human, subhuman or, for that matter, superhuman, but extends as far as does actuality itself. If, as seems reasonable, "authentic" signifies that the item of which it is predicated is genuinely what its name indicates it should be and seems to be, then the reply which equates "existence" with "be-ing actually" constitutes an existentialism which is authentic.[14]

But this authentic existentialism is also a humanism since it places individual men higher than all other existents save God because each human existent by reason of his spiritual powers of intellect and will is free, thereby fashioning a psychological individuality of subjectivity which complements his entitative individuality of supposit and nature.[15] Yet it is a theistic humanism because it culminates in acknowledging God as the efficient, final and exemplary cause that human subjects (and, for that matter, all other existents) do exist.[16] As their creator He sets forth guidelines for them to follow if they are truly to develop themselves to their full stature and attain the happiness they deserve and He intends. Freedom is, indeed, self-determination but not in the sense that each person determines what objectively is valuable[17] but that each can choose whether or not to accept the values presented to him. Freedom has to do, at bottom, with efficient and not with value-determining causality.[18] If current unauthentic or radical existentialists would listen to Thomas, their humanism would be better for it.

The fact that Aquinas' existentialism is authentic can also profit contemporary radical existentialists, as well even as non-existentialists, with reference to natural law. "Natural law" is anathema to radical existentialists who accept Sartre's dictum, "Existence precedes essence or nature," where the verb "precedes" is equivalent to "eliminates."[19] On the other hand, "natural law" can be taken in too rigid and narrow a sense by traditionalists and essentialists. What better interpretation does Thomas himself offer? In his existentialism "essence" or "nature" includes absolutely everything in someone except existence; therefore, it comprises not only a man's soul and matter (his substantial being), his faculties and their operations, the operative habits (both moral and intellectual) which perfect them, his skills; but also all his relationships—spatial, temporal, ecological, familial, civic, cultural, environmental: all these are the actual situations in which he lives, all these help constitute his *nature* (see S.T., I, 84, 7 resp.). But the natural law is founded directly upon nature; therefore, natural law is founded upon and must express all those actual and intrinsic perfections, including, yes, his substantial being (which he has in common with other people), his operative powers, habits and skills, but also his relationships (which may be uniquely his).

Thus existentially conceived, natural law remains an objective norm, based not only on the accidental but also on the substantial aspects of his being (thus it would be better than the often arbitrary and entirely subjective set of values a radical existentialist such as Sartre might elaborate for himself). But it is more concrete and flexible than more traditional and abstract conceptions of natural law because it takes into account the entire actual person—not only in his substantial being and properties but also in all his individual circumstances and situations (hence, it may offer a greater opening to individual morally justified choices in population-control and family-planning).

Aquinas' existentialism also can perhaps hold the attention even of current astrophysicists, who increasingly are beginning to ask metaphysical questions concerning existence and creation, to judge by recent news media. In *Time* for June 27, 1977, the "Science" article was entitled, "Witnesses to a Creation," where "witness" refers to an evolving star—called MWC 349—in the constellation Cygnus which is forming its own planets from the enormous glowing disc surrounding it (p. 71). On November 25, 1977, the *Chicago Tribune* carried an article entitled, "Another Clue Found to Secret of Creation"— namely, a dipotron, which is a new sort of quark. The long article, "Those Baffling Black Holes," in the "Science" section of *Time* for September 4, 1978, often speaks of "existence," as these samplings reveal. "If whole stars can vanish from sight within black holes," which figuratively are "rips in the very fabric of space and time" but more literally are mathematical figments solving the complex equations of Einstein's theory of gravity (p. 53), if those stars are "literally crushed out of existence, where has their matter gone? To another place and another time? Where did it come from? In searching for answers to the fundamental questions raised by black holes, scientists are infringing on the realm of philosophers and theologians. They are trying to find the meaning of life, of being, of the universe itself" (p. 50). A bit later in the article: "astrophysics intersects metaphysics" when the scientist studies black holes and realizes that "the gravitational collapse of stars suggests that the universe, too, can begin falling back in on itself. If that happens, its billions of galaxies will eventually crush together and would form a super black hole. And what then? Nothing? Or would a new process of creation somehow begin? (p. 54).

Finally: religion and science, as Lance Morrow observes in *Time* for February 5, 1979, "find themselves jostled into a strange metaphysical intimacy" when they agree "about certain facts concerning the creation of the universe." According to *Genesis* "the universe began in a single, flashing act of creation: the divine intellect willed all into being, *ex nihilo.*" On the other hand, an increasing number of scientists propose the "Big Bang" theory: "the universe had an instant of creation: it came to be in a vast fireball explosion 15 or 20 billion years ago. The shrapnel created by that explosion is still flying outward" to fashion the universe (p. 149). But in this apparent convergence of science and theology in the Big Bang theory of cosmogony and cosmology, has science really validated the biblical myth of creation? However one fields that question, this remains true: "the new coincidence of scientific and theological versions of creation seems to have opened up a conversation [between theologians, philosophers and scientists] that has been neglected for centuries" and that can lead to the most interesting inquiry of all: what came before the Big Bang? (p. 150).

How easily Aquinas can enter into that dialogue and what helpful insights he may contribute to it is readily gathered from the facts that his position gives primacy to actual existence: to be real is to exist; that for him God properly causes all things actually to be since His very nature is existence; that to create is efficiently and freely to cause something to exist which before was in no way; that creation is simply an exercise of God's proper causality, through which an existent universe replaces nothingness and by which beings are produced *precisely as beings* since "being" is "that which actually exists"—therefore, creation occurs on the very level of being itself, since God properly causes *being* in all beings.[20]

Finally, Aquinas has something constructive to say on a topic outside astrophysics and Einsteinian relativity but at the very center of the almost constant current concern in psychological labs and literature, in classrooms, in ecclesiastical centers, in religious and spiritual formation, in novels, contemporary theater, movies, TV soap operas. That topic is love. One need not document in any detail the omnipresent interest in and earnest attempts to practice love. Let these two quotations suffice. John Powell, S.J., the author of paperbacks on spiritual and psychological matters, of which millions of copies are sold, states in his recent *The Secret of Staying in Love* (Niles, Ill.: Argus Communications, 1974) in a section entitled "Salvation in and through love," p. 44: "More important than any psychological theory, teaching, or therapeutic technique, that which heals and promotes human change and growth is a one-to-one relationship of love." Secondly: "It is an absolute human certainty that no one can know his own beauty or perceive a sense of his own worth until it has been reflected back to him in the mirror of another loving, caring human being" (p. 55).[21]

Granted, then, the necessity of love in one's life and our contemporaries' concern about it, but what theory of Aquinas is especially apropos? His proposal that in our nonconstructural knowledge the known makes the knower, that what is known is the content-determining-cause of my spontaneous cognition. Let me explain.

According to Kant and Neokantians the knower makes the known: he applies the a priori forms of space and time and the categories of his mind to sense data, which thereby are constructed into phenomena. But one loves what one knows; but one has made what one knows; therefore, one loves what he himself has made; therefore, the object of his love is not the beloved herself but the beloved as a phenomenon constructed by himself; consequently, love of another precisely as other and in her own reality is impossible.[22]

Unselfish love flows from Aquinas' epistemological position much more facilely. For him the known makes the knower inasmuch as the known is the content-determining-cause of spontaneous cognition; but the knower loves when a good presents itself (i.e., the object of love is the good-as-known); but a good presents itself through knowledge (which is the direct result of the known affecting the knower); therefore, the good presenting itself through knowledge causes love in the knower, who thereby loves the good as it itself is and not as it is constructed by the knower. Hence, the beloved causes my love: I love a friend precisely as he is in and for himself. Love is then unselfish.

Obviously, the key to that argumentation is this: what is known is the content-determining-cause of spontaneous knowledge. Upon what does Aquinas base that proposition? Upon the brilliant insight Aristotle expresses in *On the Soul*, Book III, ch. 2, 425b26 and 426a10: "The actuation of what is sensed and of the sense is one and the same (although the being of each is not the same), but that actuation is in the sense and not in what is sensed."

If we transfer that insight from sense perception to any spontaneous knowledge, we obtain this: the actuation of what is known and of the faculty knowing is one and the same but it is present in the faculty and not in the known. It is an actuation of the known and is caused by the known, while simultaneously it also is an actuation of the knower too and, in fact, is solely *in* the knower. This is truly remarkable. The very same actuation which pre-cognitively conditions, determines, forms the faculty by being present in it (and which is the sensible or intelligible species) is also the actuation of that which is known (pre-cisely as known, though, and not as it is outside the cogni-tive process, where its actuations are its substantial and accidental forms and its act of existing) and which is caus-ing it in the knower. Through this actuation, which is *in* and *of* the knower and *of* and *from* the known, the object known is the content-determining-cause of my knowledge and, thereby, also the cause of my love. Can genuine and unselfish love of the other as other be grounded as well in a different epistemology? in a Kantian epistemology?[23]

FINAL WORDS

In answering whether Thomas can speak to contempo-rary minds, we thought it necessary to discover who those contemporaries are and, thereby, on what topics he might hope to find an audience. Having attempted that discov-ery, we must remind ourselves that Thomas is himself dead and, hence, cannot personally address the modern world. Accordingly, it is up to us: we must (so to speak) ascend the pulpit. This ascension demands that we under-stand contemporary thinkers as well as possible;[24] second-ly, that we probe Aquinas' thought as deeply and authen-tically as possible (hence, how providential is the founding of this new "Center for Thomistic Studies"!); and, finally, that through our publications, public lectures, classroom lectures and seminars, attendance at conventions and so on we disseminate his positions as widely and effectively as possible if we are to help leaven the twentieth-century world in which we live. Confronted with such an enor-mous task, I can only say: "Saint Thomas Aquinas, pray for us!" Amen.

1. The quotation from Maritain is taken from Gerald B. Phelan, "St. Thomas and the Modern Mind," *Modern Schoolman*, 20 (November, 1942): 37-47, who begins his article with references to Maritain's investigation (for publication data, see next note below).

2. Hence, the title of the book in which Maritain published the results of his investigation: *Trois Réformateurs* (Paris: Plon, 1925); English translation: *Three Reformers* (London: Sheed and Ward, 1928).

3. Phelan, art. cit., p. 37. The initial sentence is a quotation from Maritain, *Three Reformers,* p. 4.

4. See D.J. Cardinal Mercier, *Christianisme dans le monde moderne* (Paris: Perrin, 1919), p. 104.

5. The movements of thought Phelan mentions were topics for the other papers in the *Schoolman* Symposium, "Kantianism and the Modern Mind," which culminated in Phelan's paper.

6. E. Gilson, *The Unity of Philosophical Experience* (New York: Charles Scribner's Sons, 1937 and 1965), pp. 244-247. Gilson quotes Hegel from J. Loewenberg (ed.), *Hegel Selections* (New York: Charles Scribner's Sons, 1929).

7. See Gilson, *Unity*, p. ix.

8. On that success see the results of a questionnaire returned by alumni of Rockhurst College (Kansas City) and Xavier University (Cincinnati) for the years 1920 to 1960 and 1930 to 1963 respectively—*Rockhurst Alumnus*, 4 (March, 1969), p. 1: "The course of studies which alumni of every decade found to have had the most beneficial impact on their lives was that of philosophy, and this by a wide margin"; "Report on Xavier University Questionnaire on Influence of Studies," p. 2: "The heart of the questionnaire is Question X, where the respondents are asked to rank (to three places) the disciplines or branches of study that they consider to have had the most beneficial influence in their lives. Here philosophy is a very strong first both in first place votes and in weighted ranking. ...A factor worth noting is that the ratings do not correspond with the majors. Philosophy, which is rated first in influence, is tied for tenth to twelfth places as a major with education and management. It drew over eight times as many first place votes and about eighteen times as many total votes as it had majors." The philosophy then taught at both Rockhurst and Xavier would have been scholastic and, generally, thomistic.

9. Where should one put such terrorist groups as the Red Brigades of Italy, the Weathermen of the United States, the cultists?

10. See *Chicago Sun Times* for March 13, 1979. George Will's Column, © 1979, The Washington Post Company. Reprinted with permission.

11. L. Sweeney, S.J., "Gabriel Marcel's Position on God," *New Scholasticism*, 44 (1970): 111. This sort of existentialism I shall call "unauthentic" or "radical" below—see portion of this paper corresponding to note 14.

12. The quotations from Kierkegaard are from G.M. Andersen (transl.) and P.P.

Rohde (ed.), *The Diary of Søren Kierkegaard* (New York: Philosophical Library, 1960), pp. 102, 103 and 106.

13. This is Sartre's explicit position: "My freedom is the unique foundation of values. And since I am the being by virtue of whom values exist, nothing— absolutely nothing—can justify me in adopting this or that value or scale of values. As the unique basis of the existence of values, I am totally unjustifiable. And my freedom is in anguish at finding that it is the baseless basis of values." Sartre's statement is given by G. Marcel, *The Philosophy of Existentialism* (New York: Citadel Press, 1964), p. 87.

14. See L. Sweeney, S.J., "Existentialism: Authentic and Unauthentic," *New Scholasticism*, 40 (1966): 40 sqq.

15. See *ibid.*, pp. 44-52.

16. This acknowledgement occurs when one becomes aware that existence in any actual thing is a gift, and a gift indicates a Giver, who ultimately proves to be God. More fully expressed: the actuation of existence perfects the existent and yet is other than his essence, with the result that no material existent exists of its very nature; yet things do exist, do have that perfection of actuality but, as we said, not of their very nature; therefore, there must be an Existent whose very nature or essence is to exist, who of His very nature is actuality and thus needs no cause, and yet who can and does properly cause all else to exist: God, subsistent actuality. Also see L. Sweeney, S.J., "God Does Exist," *Ensign*, 1 (Spring, 1967): 5-10.

17. On Sartre's interpretation of self-determination see above, note 13.

18. This causality is a counterpart of content-determining-cause *re* knowledge. On this latter see L. Sweeney, S.J., *A Metaphysics of Authentic Existentialism* (Englewood-Cliffs, N.J.: Prentice-Hall, 1965; Ann Arbor, Michigan: Books on Demand, 1977), pp. 309-310 and 326-327.

19. On "Existence precedes essence," see *ibid.*, pp. 102-107.

20. For a discussion of creation as the production of beings as beings, see L. Sweeney, S.J., "*Esse* in Albert the Great's Texts on Creation in *Summa de Creaturis* and *Scriptum in Libros Sententiarum*," *Southwestern Journal of Philosophy*, 11 (1980), the portion of the article corresponding to note 50.

21. Powell's authorities on love are Viktor Frankl, C.G. Jung, Erich Fromm, Henry Stack Sullivan.

22. That the beloved must be the other precisely as other, see Powell, *ibid.*, pp. 64-65: "'Two solitudes that protect, touch and greet each other' (Rainer Maria Rilke). Here we find the only reality worthy of the name love. The two partners drop, however gradually, the projected image which was the first source of attraction to find the even more beautiful reality of the person. They are willing to acknowledge and respect *otherness* in each other. Each person values and tries to promote the inner vision and mysterious destiny of the other. Each counts it his privilege to assist in the growth and realization of the other's vision and destiny."

23. On Kant's influence upon radical existentialism, as well as upon British analytic philosophy, see E.L. Mascall, "The Gulf in Philosophy: Is Thomism the Bridge?", *Thomist*, 38 (January, 1974): 22: each of those theories has in common Kant's position that "the object of human knowledge is manufactured by the experiencing subject." Mascall cleverly characterizes the British philosophers as offering clarity without content, the Continental existentialists as offering content without clarity.

24. Aquinas can be our model even here. He had, as Phelan points out (art. cit., p. 42), his own *moderni*: the Latin Averroists and Avicennianizing Augustinians of the thirteenth century. Despite an occasional but rare display of strong language, he "preserved the greatest restraint in dealing with his adversaries. He never lost respect for the great minds with whom he differed but regretted, rather, that they had not been able to see the truth." And "he was scrupulous to give them credit for whatever was valuable and true in what they had to say. His works are full of references to Greek, Arabian and Jewish authors, with whose philosophy he is in thorough disagreement, but whose statements he very frequently quotes with generous approval." Such should be our attitude to our own *moderni*: in modern thought "there are likewise many valid insights. Great and powerful minds have given lifetimes to the elaboration of vast and comprehensive, though erroneous, systems. Though the history of modern philosophy is strewn with their failures, much that is perennially true lies tangled and distorted in the meshes of their thought and many fresh, though partial, visions of truth emerge through their reflections. These must not be overlooked nor should we fail in gratitude to those who have revealed them" (*ibid.*, p. 47).

The Future of Thomistic Metaphysics

Joseph Owens, C.Ss.R.

Pontifical Institute of Mediaeval Studies

I

At first reading the above title might suggest claims to a gift of prophecy. However, the future of Thomistic metaphysics is not to be looked for in any crystal ball. Neither can it be deduced with at all acceptable accuracy from the happenings of past or present. History keeps springing surprises. Rarely do things turn out exactly as predicted. This holds with especially striking force in regard to what is transmitted through writings. Books have their own fates, as the ancient Latin proverb asserts. Some *prima facie* ground is indeed provided for the observation in the sayings of Democritus that though courage sets an undertaking afoot, chance dominates in the end.[1] Chance elements are always at play. They can wreak havoc with rational prediction.

Nevertheless, for people working actively for the future of Thomistic metaphysics there is strong need to project in clearcut terms what is envisaged, with the reasons why it may be expected to occur. If I may take the liberty of applying to Thomistic metaphysics in particular what Professor Robb told us yesterday about Christian philosophy in general, "the future is the perspective from which we ought to view our task." Quest for rational pattern is imperative here, no matter what flexibility one has to allow for chance obstacles.

First and foremost, in approaching this topic, there must be confidence in the basic earnestness of philosophy and of those who give their lives to it. A recent writer has remarked: "the philosopher sees what needs doing and does it."[2] If important things need doing and can be done by the metaphysics of Aquinas better than by any other, there should be reasonable assurance that interest in his way of philosophizing will continue as long as those needs are felt. The incentive for promoting Thomistic metaphysics will be there.

The need in fact has been felt recurrently in the past. It has shown itself to be something that lasts through crises and changes of history, with sharp resurgence after periods of neglect. The need as experienced in the troubled sixteenth century prompted the *Piana* edition of Aquinas.[3] As felt in the mid-nineteenth century it occasioned wide study of his teaching and set afoot the critical edition of his works.[4] In both these respects, namely editing and understanding, the way has been opened for ample work in the future.

As regards editing, critical texts of a good part of the writings of Aquinas are already available. His commentary on the *Metaphysics* of Aristotle has recently been completed and will be in print very soon.[5] But organized work on the text of the commentary on the first two books of Lombard's *Sentences*, most important of all for a depth study of Aquinas' metaphysical thought, has not yet even commenced. The task of editing this section does not take on any precise contours in the presently visible horizon. Other works vital to the study of Aquinas' metaphysics still lack critical texts.[6] But the tremendous labor already devoted to the transmission of his writings, with volumes appearing in the last few decades at a faster rate and with higher

standards than before, seems a sufficient pledge of continued interest in making his works a permanent cultural
possession of mankind in readily accessible form.

In regard to understanding the works, the tradition of
using metaphysical passages from Aquinas' writings has
been continuous from his own time. With the fifteenth
century full scale commentaries began. Subsequently
innumerable efforts have been made to systematize his
metaphysical doctrines into textbook form. This work testifies eloquently to the enduring need for the thought of
Aquinas. Yet the situation is at the moment not too satisfactory. To a large extent, and during the last one hundred
years rather explicitly, the efforts have concentrated on
translation of Aquinas into terms intelligible to the respective historical periods. The attitude presumed seems to
have been that the metaphysical doctrines are readily discernible in Aquinas. The obstacles were located in medieval
terminology and medieval techniques. What more was
required than to present the clearly etched doctrines in
modern guise?

This policy, however, encountered its disappointments.
Interpretation so reached turned out less intelligible than
the original text, prompting the quip that if you wish to
understand Cajetan you have to read Aquinas. The
vigorous efforts of Mercier, Maritain, Gilson, Mascall and a
host of others had a history of considerable success, with
brilliant acclaim for a short time, but petering out in the last
two decades. Very little mention of Aquinas has been left
from it in widely read philosophical literature at the present
moment, and no real impact is discernible. Aquinas is
hardly playing the role of a significant thinker for the
interests of contemporary philosophy.

But even before the wave of Neoscholastic enthusiasm
had attained its latest crest, the approach from the viewpoint of translating Aquinas into modern terms had been

labeled "entirely unjustified." This critique was not meant to register pessimism, but rather satisfaction that the real situation was at last being grasped in "a growing realization of the fact that we have scarcely begun to understand the Thomistic metaphysic."[7] The first task, rather, is to penetrate the metaphysical thinking of Aquinas just as it stands in itself. This is no easy undertaking, and in it tradition can be misleading. The immediate disciples of Aquinas did not seem to have any inkling of the metaphysical aspects in his thought that have aroused the greatest interest in the present century.[8] In his traditional commentators his distinctive metaphysics seems to get lost in a run-of-the-mill Scholasticism. Actually, his own metaphysics was developed in the course of work in sacred theology. It was not envisaged as a larger logic meant to minister to the needs of particular sciences.[9] It was not a closed system, and does not prove immune to radically pluralistic interpretations.[10] Though it has been dyslogistically labeled an alternative type of rationalism,[11] it allows surprisingly full scope for the sentient and appetitive sides of human personality. It is far from what has been called an Aristotelianism rigidly imposed upon Judeo-Christian tradition.[12] It is itself, and has to be understood for what it is in its own right.

The scope of the present paper will be to take just three instances in which the metaphysical thinking of Aquinas stands out as distinctive and as meeting perennial needs of the human mind in a way not equalled by any other type of philosophy. These should be sufficient to illustrate how a study of the wants provided for by Thomistic metaphysics may be expanded into numerous other instances and present a wide and solid basis for the conclusion that there will always be a serious need for the type of thinking found in Aquinas. Could a more lasting incentive be offered towards working for the future of Thomistic metaphysics?

The present year marks the hundredth anniversary of Leo XIII's encyclical *Aeterni Patris,* urging the restoration of Aquinas as a "friendly star" for guiding human culture and progress. The centenary occurs unfortunately at a low ebb in general Thomistic interest. For the most part, teachers and writers in philosophy at the moment do not seem to like Aquinas, and students are not being attracted to him. Is this not an appropriate time, then, for focusing attention on the needs for bringing back St. Thomas to the place envisaged for him by *Aeterni Patris,* needs that require his future as a teacher of metaphysics?

II

The first area that might be signalized as having acute and permanent need for the metaphysics of Aquinas is human knowledge of the existence, nature and providence of God. Correct knowledge of God will always be necessary for man's understanding of the universe and of his own self and ultimate destiny. On the occasion of Pope John Paul II's recent visit to Poland the press was quick to point out how strongly belief in God survives even under militant atheist government. But though originating through divine revelation this belief calls for understanding and defense in the rational orbit in which man lives and thinks. No experimental or mathematical science is equipped to undertake this task. It belongs to metaphysics.

In Aquinas God is presented trenchantly in terms of existence. The things that confront us exist. Their existence is accidental and prior to them, showing that it comes from something else and ultimately from existence that subsists. It is in this manner that Aquinas interprets the traditional ways to God, expressly with Pseudo-Dionysius and demonstrably enough with other ways he accepts.[13] Actually it is but the way St. Paul declares that the invisible things of God become known through the things that are

made.[14] It is the way God is introduced in the opening
words of the Bible as he who made heaven and earth. It is
the first notion of God professed in the traditional Christian
creeds. It is the answer to the first question in the traditional
catechism. But in Aquinas it is developed through cogent
metaphysical reasoning in terms of existence, culminating
in existence itself as subsistent, personal, all-knowing, all-
powerful, provident to the smallest detail, and under
whose ever-present surveillance the life of free creatures
with its tremendous responsibilities is led. By presenting
God basically in terms of existence, Aquinas does justice
both to the negative theology in which God cannot be
conceptualized, and to the rich positive theology that fills
volumes on the divine attributes and activities.

The advantages and the need of so cogent a presentation
of God on the strictly philosophical level should be obvious
in the contemporary situation. Language about God has
been termed nonsensical or merely metaphorical. Genuine
and firm knowledge of him on the part of human reasoning
has been denied. Relation with him has been left to feeling
or mysticism. Process thinking has viewed God vaguely as
something that is gradually developing. This is a far cry
from the supreme Lord over all and personal judge to
whom all men are responsible for their actions. It is a far cry
even from Aristotle's strong statement (*Metaph.*, lambda 7,
1072b30-1073a5) that supreme beauty and goodness and
perfection are at the beginning, in divine separate substance, and not as the result of development. Even the
designation of existent has been denied to God by firm
believers who in the wake of Peirce require one to speak of
the reality of God in a sense that deliberately excludes the
obvious meaning of existence.[15]

Certainly a clear philosophical understanding of God in
the sense of the maker of heaven and earth, the God who
can give existence to everything else because he is existence

itself, is of prime importance in our present culture. In no writer does that clear and profound philosophical notion of God appear so sharply etched as in Aquinas, and so immune to conventional attacks.

There are of course hurdles in the way of general acceptance today for this presentation of God. Some serious thinkers object strongly to anything like demonstration in regard to God. They want the matter left entirely to religious belief. They seem afraid of weakness in human reasoning. One of the them has written: "The bland identification of God with the absolute or the infinite today appears to many of us as a species of idolatry," and "it is in my view a paradox to suppose that such a reality could be known or truly affirmed only on the basis of indirect evidence."[16] To see God as placed in the conclusion of a merely human demonstration, cramping him into the confines of a rationally deduced proposition, takes on the appearance of blasphemy. Aquinas, however, was well aware in this regard that no effect can have any proportion to God. Yet from any effect whatsoever the existence of a cause can be demonstrated. What results rather is that this procedure via existence cannot be expected to yield perfect knowledge of God from the viewpoint of conceptualization.[17] But it never asked that.

Others in milder fashion may just prefer to keep their religious belief separate from their reasoning. Reasoning to God may make no impression upon them compared to the vivid force of belief.[18] Quite readily the all-pervasive disagreements among philosophers may generate a practical skepticism about the power of human reason to say anything about God. The predominant Catholic tradition, nevertheless, has been that God may be known through his visible works, and that faith seeks understanding.[19] Spontaneously we want to understand as far as possible what we believe, quite in accord with the opening sentence of Aristotle's *Metaphysics* that all men by nature desire to know. The skepticism because of radical disagreements among philosophers is an objection against philosophic reasoning in general, and is explained adequately through the wide variety of starting points that confront human philosophy. Things, thought, language all offer innumerable starting points, starting points that cannot be demonstrated and once accepted cannot be refuted within the particular philosophy. If you accept the materialistic starting point that every existent has to be extended in length, breadth and thickness, you obviously will never be able to reach an immaterial being such as God. If you place your starting point exclusively in finite nature, the problem of the leap to a positively infinite nature stands in your way. The choice of the correct starting point is accordingly paramount. With Aquinas it is the existent sensible thing, obvious to all and allowing cogent metaphysical reasoning to existence that subsists. This existence, contrary to Pascal's famous remark in *Le Mémorial*, is readily shown to be the God of Abraham, the God of Isaac and the God of Jacob.[20]

Finally, it might be urged that the metaphysical reasoning of Aquinas has meaning only for the specialist, that it is over the heads of ordinary educated people and can play no role in our general culture. This objection could boomerang in the sense of showing the necessity for closer and widespread study of Aquinas in general Catholic education, the exact point of Pope Leo's encyclical. Any mind capable of studying philosophy is surely capable of understanding Aquinas, if the proper empathy and industry and instruction be brought to the task. Even though full absorption is not achieved—and after all, how many students are really on top of Plato or Kant or Hegel—does not a moderate acquaintance with the reasoning of Aquinas meet the requirement for the practical considerations of general culture? Will not this acquaintance be sufficient defense against the usually encountered attacks on the demonstration of God's existence, such as the use of the principle of causality outside sensible experience, the leap from a finite starting point to an infinite being, or the culmination in a cold primary movent that cannot by any stretch of adaptation be made to coincide with the warm loving Father revealed in the Judeo-Christian Scriptures? Even a limited acquaintance with the metaphysics of Aquinas shows at once that none of these attacks come anywhere near their target when brought to bear on his reasoning.

In a word, no matter how firm a cultured person's religious belief in God is, it naturally calls for understanding and intellectual consolidation with the world encountered in everyday life. The reasoning of St. Thomas meets this requirement cogently. Other arguments may be resorted to as having more popular appeal. With a great many people the argument known as that from universal consent may make the quickest impression.[21] But at best it is an argument from authority, and can be easily thrown into reverse. The moral argument that a man is conscious of responsibility for his actions can be pressed home with surprising force, as in Kant and Newman.[22] Yet at most it *postulates* a supreme legislator before whom men are responsible. It does not offer cogent proof that the legislator exists. The guilt feelings from which it starts are open to counter psychological explanations, against which it does not possess the means to argue satisfactorily. The ontological argument may fascinate some skillful logicians, but the majority of philosophers find it either logically erroneous or else presupposing the existence it seeks to demonstrate.[23] The great craftsman argument, which goes back to Plato, though vivid, is merely an analogy. None of these ways is acceptable in the orbit of Aquinas, no matter how much popular interest they excite.[24] Though his own procedure is much quieter, it offers effectually the deep understanding sought by the human intellect regarding the God accepted on faith. It enables the inquiring intellect to live harmoniously and joyously with the belief in the God revealed through Scripture and worshipped in sacramental dedication.

III

A second enduring need for Thomistic metaphysics regards the human soul. An entrenched mentality in contemporary culture focuses human living on the sixty to eighty good years a person may expect in the perceptual world. Christian teaching, on the other hand, directs everything to a life that matures only after soul leaves body in death. This is a touchy point in dealing with many social issues and personal problems. One has to face the icy sarcasm evoked by the sacrifice of sure and solid advantages for awaited compensation in an alleged shadowy disembodied existence. The support of cogent metaphysical underpinning for the immortality believed in through faith is certainly welcome here. Even for the world of Aristotle, where human happiness was concentrated essentially in a full lifespan on earth, there were circumstances in which a man was required to sacrifice that life for the sake of doing the right thing. Likewise today a profound moral sense may prompt a person to give up prosperity and even life itself in some situations. Naturally we want to know why. The faith gives us, in the prospect of reward in life after bodily death, an adequate motive for making the great sacrifice. Can this be sustained by reasoning on the unaided natural level?

The question may not be so simple as appears at first sight. Some people, along the lines of the mentality already considered in regard to the existence of God, would like the problem of the immortality of the soul left entirely to faith.

They prefer not to be disturbed by the invasion of reasoning into the discussion. A governor-general of Canada, the late Georges Vanier, related a conversation with one of his predecessors, Lord Byng of Vimy, about some written reflections in which Byng claimed to believe in the soul's immortality as implicitly as anyone, but to be rather pleased that nobody had ever succeeded in proving it to him! He preferred to let it remain that way, a matter of purely religious belief.[25] Similarly the arguments put by Plato (*Phaedo* 70A-107B) into the mouth of Socrates as he passed his last hour before legally decreed death in his prison cell seemed to simmer out and fade away before reaching their conclusion. This prompted a hearer to remark that the subject was so great and human weakness so notorious as to leave the answer doubtful in spite of Socrates' wholehearted conviction. Even Cardinal Cajetan, who for centuries has held the rank of leading Thomistic commentator, set aside the possibility of philosophical demonstration for the soul's immortality, on the ground that unaided human reason cannot show how the soul could perform any activity at all without sensible images present to it in a body.[26]

The word "immortality," both from its etymology and its actual use, implies life, the opposite of death. Understood in this way, it is not the immediate goal of the reasoning in Aquinas. The reasoning is that the human soul, because of its thinking in terms of universality and complete reflexion on itself, acts in a way that transcends material conditions. In consequence it has its existence in independence of the matter it informs. Its existence belongs to it as form. Once it has received being it exists necessarily and perpetually. It could no more be separated from its existence than from itself.[27] As an existent it has within itself no principle that tends towards destruction as matter does in composites. It has no orientation in itself towards non-existence. Its nature requires existence. It is naturally indestructible.

Separation from matter in death cannot cause it to perish.

That is the reasoning of Aquinas. It is not immediately a demonstration of life after death, in contradistinction to perpetual existence. What it does prove is that the spiritual soul can never perish. The soul will always be there, in existence. But because of separation from the body, it is deprived of its natural way of acting. From what we know of its nature there does not seem to be any metaphysically cogent reason that would show vital activity on its part after death. But just as little can the possibility of elevation to preternatural ways of acting be ruled out. Aquinas himself has not the least doubt on that score. The notion of a substance continuing in existence without any activity is abhorrent to him. It would have no purpose for its existence.[28]

Perhaps nobody will have any real difficulty in following this reasoning of Aquinas from existent substance to accompanying activity. But the question has in fact been raised in periodical literature. Moreover, in the metaphysics of Aquinas no creature is immediately operative. For him a finite substance is of itself an immediate potentiality only towards existence. All its potentialities towards activity are accidents added to it and really distinct from it.[29] Human reasoning can show that the soul is by its nature indestructible. The soul will continue to exist forever after bodily death. But unaided human reasoning does not show any natural potentiality in the soul for activity apart from the sensible images that require union with the body for their functioning. Unaided reasoning can accordingly demonstrate the perpetual existence of the soul without being required to prove metaphysically the fact of life after death. That can be left to faith. There is no need to fall back on unsatisfactory arguments that attractive though they may be do not succeed any more than they did with Socrates in convincing the hearers. Likewise one can grant Cajetan's point that unaided reason cannot show how a soul can have vital activity apart from the body, and yet accept as cogent Aquinas' demonstration of the soul's indestructibility. That is the metaphysical underpinning required here.

IV

The third need concerns the destiny of man, the purpose of human living. Aquinas approaches this question with the Christian belief that the ultimate purpose of a man's life is the beatific vision of God. That vision is eternal life. Human destiny consists entirely in that contemplation of the divinity. In a word, what a man has been created for is contemplation. The only thing in which he can ultimately find his happiness is the eternal contemplation of the divine nature.

For Aquinas, trained as he was by sensitive contact with the Aristotelian ethics, there was nothing peculiar or weak about this teaching of the Scriptures. Aristotle had shown clearly that the highest happiness of man consisted in the exercise of his highest faculty on the highest possible object. For Aristotle the contemplation took place during a man's lifespan on earth. For Aquinas, this presented no difficulty, since contemplation on earth was part of a way (*via*) towards eternal contemplation after death. So for him there was nothing the least bit odd about the Scriptural direction of all human living towards perpetual contemplation.

For the ordinary man today, however, this view may not seem so enticing. It seems a rather wan and thin-blooded notion of life. People want to be active, they want to do things, to make money, to improve the social and political orders, to engage in sports, travel and hundreds of varied activities. Eternal contemplation would seem like a continued watching of television (getting sleepier and sleepier all the time) instead of active engagement in life—and even with television there is incessant change of scenes, while in the beatific vision there is eternally the one unchanging object. The prospect would seem rather bleak. The need for the Marthas is palpable, but for the Marys, very Apollonian.

This is a crucial problem, when one considers that it bears on the purpose for which everything is done in one's life. In no other philosophy are the issues involved made as clear and convincing as they are in the thought of Aquinas. For him, in the wake of Aristotle, cognition is a way of being. In cognition a man becomes and is the things he knows. In this way he possesses them all within himself (*De veritate*, II 2c). The way they exist in his sensible experience is of course inferior to the way they exist in themselves. Hence the notion of cognitional existence as allegedly wan and unreal. But prior to their existence in themselves is their existence in the divine creative essence. There they are identified with the creative essence itself, and accordingly exist in it in the highest possible way.[30] It is in that way they are possessed by human cognition in the beatific vision of God. The way all things are possessed and lived in the direct contemplation of the divine nature appears much more real and vivid and full-blooded in comparison with existence in the sensible universe, than does the sensible existence itself in comparison with existence in human cognition. The metaphysics of Aquinas explains tellingly on the level of human reason why the contemplation of God's essence, in accord with revealed doctrine, is what alone can fully satisfy human aspirations and which alone provides the ultimate goal for which a man should strive in every action.

Further, the Thomistic explanation of cognition as the existence of the thing in the percipient or the knower, shows how external things can be epistemologically first. Only through them, and in terms of them conceptually, does a man become aware of his cognition and of himself. The ever-baffling problem of passage from thought to external things does not even arise. There never was any imprisonment within cognition. From the epistemological standpoint the external things have always been first. The basic human certainty that other things and other persons exist in the world around us is given its full philosophical justification.

V

These are three outstanding areas that will continue in the future to need the metaphysics of Aquinas—God, soul, cognition. No other metaphysics yet developed will meet their needs so satisfactorily. Numerous similar needs may be catalogued as one goes through other areas in confrontation with Aquinas philosophical thinking—moral reasoning, truth, goodness, freedom, divine presence, natural law, and so on. His thought is wide open to new developments of culture and learning. It is perfectly at home with all that is worthwhile in them. It is adept at integrating them on its own level into the general pattern of human life.

Lessons, of course, are to be learned from the mistakes and shortcomings of the past in handling Thomistic metaphysics. Work in the sphere of the particular sciences cannot be expected of it. Nor can it be looked upon as a system, neat and fixed, and merely handed down from one generation to another. Rather, the philosophical thinking of Aquinas has to be lived anew by each thinker who would profit by it. It will be different in each individual who absorbs its influence and inspiration. One has to get used to this live pluralism if the thought of Aquinas is to play an effective role. The ways of understanding him may be expected to vary as individually as fingerprints, yet with "family resemblances"[31] that mark them clearly as Thomistic in character. By the same token, the thought of Aquinas will lose somewhat in each commentator who undertakes to teach it or interpret it. Part of it keeps escaping in the processes of transmission, like nitrogen liquified for transport. To be fully effective it has to be learned from the writings of Aquinas himself. Taken live from that source, the needs for it should assure its future.

One hundred years ago the *Aeterni Patris* designated Aquinas as the *princeps*[32] of Catholic thinkers. Yet the recent *aggiornamento* in the Church has not based itself in very explicit fashion upon his thought. In fact in its earlier stages during the sixties there was much open revolt against him. Might not the reason be that it still has not come to grips with the deep philosophical issues? Some fifteen years ago an editorial in *America* noted that while an extensive variety of other disciplines had been taking their part in the *aggiornamento*, the most explosive role may be expected to be played by what had been entirely neglected, the "issue of philosophy."[33] That challenge still remains open. In any case, the needs just considered in the broader area of general culture will persist. Is that not enough to guarantee the future of Thomistic metaphysics? It is, provided the necessary care is taken to understand Aquinas correctly. His thought is transmitted to us in books, and the fate of books rests on the capacity of their readers to comprehend them.[34] Correct understanding is paramount for the continuance of his metaphysical influence on the future.

1. "Courage is action's beginning, but chance dominates the end." Fr. 269 (DK).

2. J.Q. Urmson, *Philosophical Analysis* (Oxford: Clarendon Press, 1956), p. 200.

3. For a general survey of the history, see James A. Weisheipl, in *New Catholic Encyclopedia*, s.v. "Thomism, 1," and "Scholasticism, 3." On the printing of the Piana edition, see Gian Ludovico Masetti Zannini, "Intorno all'edizione Romana delle opere di S. Tommaso (1569-1571)," *Studi Thomistici*, ed. Antonio Piolanti (Rome: Pontificia Accademia Romana di S. Tommaso d'Aquino, 1974), I: 285-290.

4. On the background in the times of Pius IX, see Antonio Piolanti, *Pio IX e la renascità del Tomismo* (Vatican City: Libreria Editrice Vaticana, 1974). This was published also in the form of an article in *Studi Thomistici*, I: 338-436. Further

studies on the background may be seen in *Saggi sulla renascità del Tomismo nel secolo XIX*, ed. Antonio Piolanti (Vatican City: Libreria Editrice Vaticana, 1974). See also Giovanni Felici Rossi, *La filosofia nel Collegio Alberoni e il neotomismo* (Piacenza: Collegio Alberoni, 1959), and *Il movimento neotomista piacentino iniziato al Collegio Alberoni da Francesco Grassi nel 1751 e la formazione di Vincento Buzzetti* (Vatican City: Libreria Editrice Vaticana, 1974).

5. This is the information given me by the editor of the volume, Professor James P. Reilly.

6. E.g., *De potentia* and other *Quaestiones disputatae, Quaestiones quodlibetales, In de anima, In Boethii De hebdomadibus*, etc.

7. "...an entirely unjustified notion that the task of the Thomist today is to translate St. Thomas into modern terms rather than to try to understand him. Fortunately there is a growing realization of the fact that we have scarcely begun to understand the Thomistic metaphysic, and that the first task of modern Thomism is to study the text patiently and receptively, returning to it again and again." Dermot O'Donoghue, "An Analysis of the *Tertia Via* of St. Thomas," *The Irish Theological Quarterly*, 20 (1953): 129.

8. On this difference in interest, see Frederick J. Roensch, *Early Thomistic School* (Dubuque: The Priory Press, 1964), pp. 315-317. Roensch notes in particular that "the most significant characteristic of a modern Thomist, (the Thomistic notion of *esse*), was not treated *ex professo* in the Middle Ages." Ibid., p. 315. Similarly the notion of the human person, about which so much has been gathered recently from the writings of Aquinas, was not a central point of interest in the earlier times, yet "it remains open to all the achievements of human thought, which have from various sides amplified the conception of the person evolved by Thomism and also have confirmed its realistic character." Karol Wojtyla, "The Structure of Self-determination as the Core of the Theory of the Person," in *Tommaso d'Aquino nel suo VII centenario, Atti del Congresso Internazionale*, no. 7 (Naples: Edizioni Domenicane Italiane, 1978), p. 43.

9. "...alicui particulari scientiae, in quibus peccatum accidit, nisi ex propriis procedatur." Aquinas, *In Boethii De trinitate*, VI, 1c (no. 1), ed. Decker, p. 205. 14-15. Cf. use of "intelligentia peccat" in *Aeterni Patris, Acta Sanctae Sedis*, XII: 98.

10. This situation may be found documented in my article "Aquinas on Knowing Existence," *Review of Metaphysics*, 29 (1976): 670-690.

11. Cf.: "...that ancient form of rationalism, Thomism"—R.A. Naulty, "A Capacity that Surpasses Human Understanding," *The Monist*, 59 (1976): 507. Accepting rationalistic procedure, however, does not at all mean doing away with any of the *sources* of intellection: "Yet it seems to me unlikely that metaphysicians attempting to be rational can be dispensed with...Possibly we need to devote more time to meditation and less (though at present it is no vast amount) to rationalistic metaphysics." Charles Hartshorne, "Mysticism and Rationalistic Metaphysics," ibid., p. 469. "Rationalism" here does not

coincide with the nineteenth century's opposition to faith.

12. "They had to impose on Gothic evangelical inspiration the deforming tyranny of Aristotelianism." José Ortega y Gasset, *Man and Crisis*, trans. Mildred Adams (New York, 1958), p. 118. On the "twenty-four theses" as "a phenomenon of a particular kind of Italian neo-Thomism," see Thomas J.A. Hartley, *Thomistic Revival and the Modernist Era* (Toronto: University of St. Michael's College, 1971), p. 59.

13. See *In I Sent.*, d. 3, div. lae partis textus, ed. Mandonnet, I, 88. On the same interpretation for each of the "Five Ways" of the *Summa theologiae*, see discussion in my article "Aquinas and the Five Ways," *The Monist*, 58 (1974): 16-35. The consideration of intermediate causes of existence is an integral part of the demonstration as found in Aquinas, and does not at all weaken the validity of the argument because "God is the *direct* cause of my finite existence here and now," as claimed by George A. Blair, "Another Look at St. Thomas' 'First Way,'" *International Philosophical Quarterly*, 16 (1976): 314. In point of fact the existence immediately experienced does come from secondary causes. Only after subsistent existence has been demonstrated can one show that the secondary agents are causing existence through the concurrence of the first efficient cause.

14. Rom., I, 20. In *Aeterni Patris*, ASS, XII: 99.

15. See Charles Sanders Peirce, *Collected Papers*, 6.495. John E. Smith in his commentary in *God, Man and Philosophy*, ed. Carl W. Grindell (New York: St. John's University, 1971), p. 60, defends Peirce's use·of the terms on the supposition that the term "existence" has been "totally captured by philosophers" to the finite meaning. One may doubt if this capture has been so total. Existentialism and realism still mean two different things. Especially in the context of Aquinas, where the distinction between *res* and *esse* is so strong, the notion of "reality" cannot be substituted for the notion of "existence" without intolerable confusion of thought.

16. Charles Hartshorne, "Present Prospects for Metaphysics," *The Monist*, 47 (1963): 190; "Mysticism and Rationalistic Metaphysics," *The Monist*, 59 (1976): 463.

17. "...ex quocumque effectu potest manifeste nobis demonstrari Deum esse, licet per eos non perfecte possimus eum cognoscere secundum suam essentiam." Aquinas, *ST*, I, 2, 2, ad 3m. Cf. "...Deus, formationem [=conceptualization] intellectus nostri subterfugit." *In III Sent.*, d. 24, a. 2, q. 3, Solut. 1, ed. Moos, III: 768 (no. 51).

18. E.g.: "The metaphysical proofs of God are so far away from the reasoning of men, and so involved, that they make little impression; and in the cases where this might give help to some people, it would do so only during the instant they are seeing the demonstration itself." Pascal, *Pensées*, *543 (ed. Brunschvicg numeration). Cf. Gabriel Marcel, *The Mystery of Being*, trans. René Hague (London: Harvill Press, 1951), II: 174-176.

19. Anselm, *Proslogium*, Proem.

20. E.g.: "What Thomas describes is clearly not the God of Job, nor the God of Abraham, Isaac, and Jacob." Walter Kaufmann, *Critique of Religion and Philosophy* (New York: Harper, 1958), p. 135; cf. pp. 115-116. "...not an abstract Prime Mover or First Cause, but a God who is interested in men of flesh and blood." H.R. Richards, "The Word of God Incarnate," *Life of the Spirit*, 13 1958): 98. A speaker from the floor called attention to the way metaphysical objects can stir the emotions. This certainly holds in regard to subsistent existence, "this truth sublime" (Aquinas, *CG*, I, 22, Hanc autem), which contains within itself in highest fashion every perfection found in creatures (cf. infra, n. 30).

21. For a history of the argument, see Paul Edwards, *Encyclopedia of Philosophy*, s.v. "Common Consent Arguments for the Existence of God." The persistence of this argument through the centuries seems to indicate the mutual support men seek from each other in questions that are remote from immediate sensible experience and where "it is lonely on the top of the mountain." Aquinas, however, does not lean on this crutch in regard to the existence of God. There is no full-length study of the argument, Edwards notes.

22. See John Henry Walgrave, "La preuve de l'existence de Dieu par la conscience morale et l'expérience des valeurs," in *L'existence de Dieu*, ed. le collège dominicain de théologie à La Sarte-Huy (Tournai: Casterman, 1961), pp.

23. See *The Ontological Argument*, ed. Alvin Plantinga (Garden City, N.Y.: Doubleday, 1965). This argument also has been put into reverse by J.N. Findlay, ibid., pp. 111-122. For Aquinas either way of arguing (i.e., either to existence or non-existence) from *what* a thing (even infinite or greater than which none can be thought) *is*, would be invalid. For him (*De ente et essentia*, c. III, ed. Roland-Gosselin, p. 26.1-10) the nature as such involves neither existence nor non-existence.

24. For objections against limiting the philosophical approach to that of efficient causality, see John E. Smith, op. cit., pp. 55-56. Smith, however, seems to allow that it is the stand of Aquinas. On the *immediacy* of God to human knowledge (Smith, pp. 56-58), the answer of Aquinas seems given in *ST*, I, 2, 1, ad 1m—it is a confused cognition in which the divine is not distinguished from other natures.

25. Robert Speaight, *Vanier*, (Toronto: Collins, 1970), p. 124.

26. On Cajetan's objection at the Fifth Lateran Council to the part of the document that on this point required of philosophers that "publice persuadendo doceant veritatem fidei," see Mansi, *Sacrorum Conciliorum Nova et Amplissimo Collectio*, 32, col. 843D. The conclusion reached by Kenneth L. Schmitz, "The Problem of the Immortality of the Human Soul in the Works of Cajetan," University of Toronto dissertation (1952), p. 381, after a careful study of the texts, is: "The texts also suggest that even in his earlier years Cajetan did not hold as apodeictic the proofs of the immortality which he later adjudged only probable." An opposite view is: "...it is true that in the last six years of his life Cajetan denied the demonstrability of personal immortality. Up to these last six years there is no evidence of such an opinion." John P. Reilly, *Cajetan's Notion of Existence* (The Hague: Mouton, 1971), p. 100. The deeper issue,

however, is that Cajetan's understanding of existence, as examined in Etienne Gilson's "Cajetan et l'existence," *Tijdschrift voor philosophie*, 15 (1953): 267-286, does not seem open to Aquinas' argument for the perpetual existence of the spiritual soul.

27. Aquinas, *ST*, I, 75, 6c. Cf. *De pot.*, V, 3c; *Q. de an.*, 14c.

28. Aquinas, *Quodl.*, III, 9, 1c: *Q. de an.*, 15c; 20c. On the problem of distinguishing the immortality of the soul from its perpetual existence in the metaphysics of Aquinas, see John F. McCormick, "Quaestiones Disputandae," *The New Scholasticism*, 13 (1939): 368-374; George St. Hilaire, "Does St. Thomas Really Prove the Soul's Immortality?" ibid., 34 (1960): 340-356. The latter seeks the solution in the experience of immortality in the present life: "If we have knowledge, if we know an *esse perpetuum*, are we not experiencing immortality? Is this not a knowledge here and now that our soul is exercising a life which is atemporal and aspatial?" (ibid., p. 352). The author goes further in maintaining: "This experiential, inductive approach, which we feel is latent in the Angelic Doctor's works and which we have attempted to unfold, is the bridge across the chasm separating materialistic anthropology from Christian philosophy" (ibid., p. 355).

    There is, of course, no doubt in the thinking of Aquinas that we immediately experience universality in cognition, transcending space and time. But for Aquinas, as already noted, that is only a premise for reasoning to the *existence* of the soul in a way that transcends the material conditions. Nothing further seems allowed from the text quoted by St. Hilaire on p. 345, n. 15: "Consequitur ergo homo perpetuitatem secundum animam" (*CG*, II, 79, Amplius impossibile). This is still far from an immediate experience of eviternity in the present life. Reasoning from experience of universality is required.

    In regard to a question from the floor on the existence of the separated soul outside time, the answer in Aquinas is to be sought in his threefold conception of duration as eternity, eviternity (*aevum*) and time, with eternity as the basic measure: "Unde sicut divinum esse est mensura omnis actus, ita aeternitas est mensura omnis durationis, excedens et non coaequata." *In I Sent.*, d. 19, q. 2, a. 1, ad 2m, ed. Mandonnet, I: 469. Cf. Solut., pp. 466-468, and *In II Sent.*, d. 2, q. 1. a. 1, Solut.; II: 62-64.

29. Aquinas, *In I Sent.*, d. 3, q. 4, a. 2, Solut. (I, 116); *ST*, I, 77, 1c: *Q. de an.*, 12.

30. Aquinas, Quodl., VIII, 1, 1c.

31. This metaphor was used by Maurice De Wulf in regard to the medieval Scholastics and appeared in English translation as early as 1907. See De Wulf, *An Introduction to Scholastic Philosophy*, trans. Peter Coffey (New York: Dover Publications, 1956), p. 46.

32. *Aeterni Patris*, ASS, XII: 108; 109. Cf. p. 118.

33. T.N. Davis, "Of Many Things," *America*, 112 (June 12, 1965): 841.

34. "Pro captu lectoris habent sua fata libelli." Terentianus Maurus, *De Litteris, Syllabis et Metris Horatii*, I: 1286, ed. Henricus Keil, *Grammatici Latini* (Hildesheim: Georg Olms, 1961), VI: 363.

Epilogue

The New Center and The Intellectualism of St. Thomas

(An Address Given at the Symposium Dinner, October 5, 1979)

Vernon J. Bourke

Center for Thomistic Studies, University of St. Thomas

We are meeting here because the late Professor Anton C. Pegis planned it. Of course there are others who gave impetus to this new philosophy program: Hugh Roy Marshall envisioned and strongly supported it; the administrative officers of the University of St. Thomas have given it their full cooperation: all members of the present department of philosophy have welcomed such a Center; and above all Father Victor Brezik has had the vision and perseverance needed to keep it going.

But Tony Pegis dreamed of a center of graduate studies in which the thought of Thomas Aquinas would be thoroughly investigated under his able direction. He even made plans for this dinner. Shortly after his death in the spring of 1978, I was asked to help with the continuation of preliminary planning for the Center for Thomistic Studies. My reluctant agreement to do so was motivated by my long association with Pegis and by my longer and greater debt to the Basilian priests who were my first teachers at the University of Toronto.

Doctor Pegis had chosen the title for this talk. When I first read the "intellectualism" of St. Thomas in his title, I thought that he was neatly avoiding saying either the philosophy or the theology of Aquinas. But there was more to Pegis' emphasis on "intellectualism" than that: for, in a memorandum that he wrote for Father Brezik in January 1976, he said (and I will read about two pages from this unpublished explanation by Pegis):

Some fifty years ago, Catholic universities were teaching philosophy with a dogmatic dedication to truth, to St. Thomas Aquinas and to the guidance of theology. The dominant aim was to teach philosophical truth 'according to the mind of St. Thomas Aquinas.' Since St. Thomas was a theologian, this attitude in time raised a question. What, then, was the difference between teaching theology and teaching philosophy? Philosophy was a free intellectual inquiry, it was argued, and could not be taught dogmatically as theology was. Mainly after the second World War, the dogmatic teaching of philosophy was succeeded, partly under the pressure of criticism (both hostile and benign) and partly under the influence of a new generation of teachers (coming to Catholic departments of philosophy from many intellectual climates), with a more pluralistic attitude toward the teaching of philosophy. The question today is: if dogmatism tends to stifle inquiry, does not pluralism tend to obscure truth? The question is a serious one, particularly for the health and direction of a new graduate school of philosophy that is anxious, within its Catholic setting, to profit from the experiences of its predecessors. Philosophy, wherever it is taught, *is* a free intellectual inquiry, open and unafraid of the search for truth. But does this free inquiry mean that men cannot find the truth except provisionally and tentatively, or does it mean that man's intellectual life is itself an inquiry, and that he can discover truth slowly, with effort and amid many adventures? Espousing the latter view, the present writer [Pegis] believes in philosophical inquiry rather than in philosophical dogmatism, but in an inquiry that is headed toward truth, and that finds in truth both freedom and an impulse toward further inquiry. I believe that such an attitude toward philosophical truth is teachable and that it has in St. Thomas Aquinas its greatest master. Here the hazards and the opportunities begin. I can say for myself that I accept St. Thomas as my philosophical teacher for two reasons that are decisive for me as a Christian and as a teacher of philosophy. The first is St. Thomas' conception of the human intellect; the second is his conception of the highest human activity of that intellect.... St. Thomas believed that man's intellect could function properly only if it followed its own native light and principles. God, he said, was the author of that intellect (and its principles) as much as he was the author of revelation. This ought to mean that, even in the world of faith, the intellect can find nothing to oppose its inner light. Men, certainly, may act (and think) darkly and perversely; but this is what they do with their light, it is not how their light itself shines. So St. Thomas believed, and this faith is the charter of an open intellectualism within Christianity itself....[1]

This is the end of the excerpt from Pegis' plan for the St. Thomas Center. May I simply say that I wholly agree with what he wrote? Indeed he was stressing what Aquinas had said at the beginning of his *Summa contra Gentiles*.[2]

Now the end of each thing is that which is intended by its first author or mover. But the first author and mover of the universe is an intellect (*est intellectus*), as will be shown later [I.44]. The ultimate end of the universe must, therefore, be the good of an intellect. This good is truth.

In what follows let us consider, very briefly, four questions: 1) Why establish a Center for Thomistic Studies here? 2) What are the special characteristics of Thomas Aquinas as a thinker? 3) How should twentieth-century scholars approach Thomism? and 4) What may the Center for Thomistic Studies accomplish?

First of all, as to why we should start such a program here, it is rather obvious that there is a lack of such centers in this country. There are many excellent graduate departments of philosophy, of course, but I do not know of any with the concentration that is planned here. If there are others, then we welcome their cooperation and wish them all success. Pegis was right when he mentioned the pluralism of many departments in the major Catholic universities in the United States. Since the early sixties there has been a decrease of interest in Thomism at Catholic seminaries, colleges and universities. In spite of this the world-wide study of the thought of Aquinas has grown apace. I am working now on a *Thomistic Bibliography* for the past forty years; it will be limited to 5000 items. We are having no trouble finding more than that many studies; our problem is what may profitably be excluded. In the Centenary year (1974), more than 2500 articles and books were published. Moreover, as Hugh Roy Marshall observed several years ago, in today's world there is a great need for a philosophy that is affirmative rather than negatively critical, that has at least some acceptable answers to ultimate questions, and that has some positive relevance to life in the twentieth century. The dominant philosophies of our day, dialectical materialism, linguistic analysis, phenomenological existentialism and quasi-scientific naturalism, take but partial views of reality and the values basic to decent human living. Many of us think that the original Thomism, re-thought in the light of present-day realities and problems, can become a useful guide for contemporary thinkers.

Secondly, what are Aquinas' distinctive credentials as a thinker? Cardinal Newman once listed the attributes of a philosophical habit of mind as, "freedom, equitableness, calmness, moderation, and wisdom."[3] Now Newman unfortunately never read the major writings of Thomas Aquinas but he did come rather close to describing the thoughtful personality of the man from Aquino. Certainly Thomas was distinguished for his moderation, for avoiding extremes. Certainly too, he was free in his search for truth: the introductions to his great works speak eloquently of his desire to break the shackles of an earlier, hidebound, academicism. Thomas' open-mindedness is evident in his extensive use of the writings of pagans, Moslems, Jews and Greek Christian thinkers. All of this is combined with a healthy respect for his predecessors in the intellectualism of Latin Christianity. If ever there was a man who exemplified St. Anselm's motto, "faith seeking understanding," St. Thomas was he. The last characteristic that I would stress is his clarity of presentation: Thomas really avoided meaningless jargon, his explanations are frequently profound but always understandable.

My third question was: How should we approach Thomism today? Broadly speaking there are two ways of studying the thought of Thomas Aquinas. The first and very necessary way involves reading his works in the best editions available and with as much understanding as one can muster, situating his thought in its historical context, and attempting to get at his own precise meanings. This is the historical-textual approach so highly developed in the school that Etienne Gilson headed and in which Anton Pegis was a leading scholar. I say that this historical approach is still necessary today, despite all the wonderful work that has followed *Aeterni Patris*. The fact of the matter is that too many people still misinterpret Aquinas nowadays. A recent book by an American Jesuit, Joseph F. Costanzo,[4] accuses Hans Küng of serious mistakes in regard to St. Thomas' handling of Greek theologies in his *Contra errores Graecorum*. A book on Christ by Eduard Schillebeeckx[5] criticizes St. Thomas' Christology in unwarranted terms. Just last month I ran across an Italian article[6] which accuses Walter Ullman, M.D. Chenu, Karl Rahner and Jacques Maritain of "deforming" Aquinas' political philosophy. Now I wouldn't send a student to either Hans Küng or Schillebeeckx for an interpretation of a Thomistic text, but the last group of scholars surely couldn't all be wrong in the same way. The point is that we still have a lot to do even to recover what St. Thomas knew in his day.

But the second, and generally more difficult, approach to Thomism involves rethinking his thirteenth-century wisdom in the light of twentieth-century realities. I do not propose to waste your time with an explanation of how different our century is from the time of St. Thomas. Let us admit that you cannot expect to find simple solutions to our present problems by looking up key-words in the text of Aquinas. What is needed in this second approach is a really philosophical and up-to-date search for the best answers available today.

Very important to such a search is a framework of discourse that is clear and understandable. Much teaching of philosophy today incorporates the reading of selections from a number of prominent thinkers, all of whom differ in the meanings that they give to basic terms, such as reason, intellect, judgment, willing, existing—and so on. It is not possible to achieve coherent understanding, if one is continually shifting from one frame of reference to another. Some philosophers take reality to be fundamentally mental in character and they deny that physical things are really there. Others deny the existence of mental realities and claim that thinking and feeling are merely bodily motions in the structure of the brain. Now you can't intelligently agree with both mentalists and materialists, for they are in mutual contradiction. These are the kinds of extreme positions that Thomas avoided. He was not necessarily correct in all his views but his broad way of looking at things (what the Germans used to call a *Weltanschauung*) was internally consistent and intelligible. Such a basic intellectual framework can easily be learned. It enables thinkers to discuss, communicate their notions to each other and to their students, in a manner that is not possible in the Babel of present-day philosophies. I would hope that the graduates and scholars at the Center for Thomistic Studies would emerge from the program well able to understand each other and to communicate such an intellectual grasp to other people.

This brings me to the last question: What can such a Center really accomplish? Most importantly it may, as I have just suggested, provide one type of sound philosophy for the coming century. This should not be a dogmatism, accepted because the Pope approved it, or because St. Thomas originated it, or for any other reason extraneous to philosophic understanding. Despite the many differences in our personal experiences and ways of using our intellects, there are some dependable truths about existing realities and the functions of mankind—and about the best ways of living a good life. Different words can be used to express such truths but the ultimate truths are not relative. It is our grasp of them that is always somewhat imperfect.

In the second place, I can foresee possible spin-offs from the philosophical research to be done at this Center—into theology, intellectual history, Church history, physical and social sciences, and politico-legal theory. Whether such developments come about will depend on the reactions of other scholars, here and elsewhere.

I would hope, too, that we might spark a new spirit of scholarship and scientific excellence in other Catholic institutions of learning. Some years ago I made a never-published study of eminent Catholic scholars and where they had done their graduate work. Most of their advanced studies were made at non-Catholic universities. Now we don't want students to avoid the great secular universities but surely there is room for improvement in the graduate work now being done under Catholic auspices. Perhaps the courses to be started here next September will help to set a higher standard of excellence.

Finally, I can see the possibility of a more distinctive educational emphasis for the University of St. Thomas and for the City of Houston. This City is already the focal point for many outstanding institutions of learning and research. St. Thomas is a relatively new and small university —yet its potentialities are limitless. There is room in this City, in this State, in this Country, and in this World, for the sort of program that we are inaugurating tonight.

1. From: "Toward A New Graduate Philosophy Program at the University of St. Thomas," by Anton C. Pegis, dated 2 January 1976.

2. I, 1, #2.

3. See Russell Kirk's discussion of these in *Modern Age*, 23, (1979): 226-231.

4. Joseph F. Costanzo, *The Historical Credibility of Hans Küng* (N. Quincy, Mass., 1978).

5. Eduard Schillebeeckx, *Jezus* (Bruges, 1974).

6. Marco Tangheroni, "Diformazioni e travisamenti del pensiero de S. Tommaso," *Rivista di Letteratura e di Storia Ecclesiastica*, 6 (1974): 65-80.

AETERNI PATRIS
ENCYCLICAL LETTER ON THE RESTORATION OF CHRISTIAN PHILOSOPHY

August 4, 1879
Pope Leo XIII

The only-begotten Son of the Eternal Father, who came on earth to bring salvation and the light of divine wisdom to men, conferred a great and wonderful blessing on the world when, about to ascend again into heaven, He commanded the apostles to go and teach all nations,[1] and left the Church which He had founded to be the common and supreme teacher of the peoples. For men, whom the truth had set free, were to be preserved by the truth; nor would the fruits of heavenly doctrines, by which salvation comes to men, have long remained had not the Lord Christ appointed an unfailing authority for the instruction of the faithful. And the Church built upon the promises of its own divine Author, whose charity it imitated, so faithfully followed out His commands that its constant aim and chief wish was this: to teach true religion and contend forever against errors. To this end assuredly have tended the incessant labors of individual bishops; to this end also the published laws and decrees of Councils, and especially the constant watchfulness of the Roman Pontiffs, to whom, as successors of the blessed Peter in the primacy of the apos-

173

tles, belongs the right and office of teaching and confirming their brethren in the faith. Since, then, according to the warning of the Apostle, the minds of Christ's faithful are apt to be deceived and the integrity of the faith to be corrupted among men *by philosophy and vain deceit*,[2] the supreme pastors of the Church have always thought it their duty to advance, by every means in their power, science truly so called, and at the same time to provide with special care that all studies should accord with the Catholic faith, especially philosophy, on which a right apprehension of the other sciences in great part depends. Indeed, venerable brethren, on this very subject among others, we briefly admonished you in our first encyclical letter; but now, both by reason of the gravity of the subject and the condition of the time, we are again compelled to speak to you on the mode of taking up the study of philosophy which shall respond most fitly to the true faith, and at the same time be most consonant with the dignity of human knowledge.

Whoso turns his attention to the bitter strifes of these days and seeks a reason for the troubles that vex public and private life must come to the conclusion that a fruitful cause of the evils which now afflict, as well as of those which threaten us, lies in this: that false conclusions concerning divine and human things, which originated in the schools of philosophy, have crept into all the orders of the state, and have been accepted by the common consent of the masses. For since it is in the very nature of man to follow the guide of reason in his actions, if his intellect sins at all his will soon follows; and thus it happens that looseness of intellectual opinion influences human actions and perverts them. Whereas, on the other hand, if men be of sound mind and take their stand on true and solid principles, there will result a vast amount of benefits for the public and private good. We do not, indeed, attribute such force and authority to philosophy as to esteem it equal to the task of combating and rooting out all errors; for, when the Christian religion was first constituted, it came upon earth to restore it to its primeval dignity by the admirable light of faith, diffused not by persuasive words of human wisdom, but in the manifestation of spirit and of power[3]; so also at the present time we look above all things to the powerful help of Almighty God to bring back to a right understanding the minds of men and dispel the darkness of error. But the natural helps with which the grace of the divine wisdom, strongly and sweetly disposing all things, has supplied the human race are neither to be despised nor neglected, chief among which is evidently the right use of philosophy. For not in vain did God set the light of reason in the human mind; and so far is the super-added light of faith from extinguishing or lessening the power of the intelligence that it completes it rather, and by adding to its strength renders it capable of greater things.

Therefore divine Providence itself requires that in calling back the peoples to the paths of faith and salvation, advantage should be taken of human science also—an approved and wise practice which history testifies was observed by the most illustrious Fathers of the Church. They, indeed, were wont neither to belittle nor undervalue the part that reason had to play, as is summed up by the great Augustine when he attributes to this science "that by which the most wholesome faith is begotten,...is nourished, defended, and made strong."[4]

In the first place, philosophy, if rightly made use of by the wise, in a certain way tends to smooth and fortify the road to true faith, and to prepare the souls of its disciples for the fit reception of revelation; for which reason it is well called by ancient writers sometimes a stepping-stone to the Christian faith,[5] sometimes the prelude and help of Christianity,[6] sometimes the Gospel teacher.[7] And assuredly the God of all goodness, in all that pertains to divine things, has not only manifested by the light of faith those truths which human intelligence could not attain of itself, but others also not altogether unattainable by reason, that by the help of divine authority they may be made known to all at once and without any admixture of error. Hence it is that certain truths which were either divinely proposed for belief, or were bound by the closest chains to the doctrine of faith, were discovered by pagan sages with nothing but their natural reason to guide them, were demonstrated and proved by becoming arguments. *For*, as the Apostle says, *the invisible things of him, from the creation of the world, are clearly seen, being understood by the things that are made: his eternal power also and divinity*[8]; and the Gentiles who have not the law show, nevertheless, the work of the law written in their hearts.[9] But it is most fitting to turn these truths, which have been discovered by the pagan sages even, to the use and purposes of revealed doctrine, in order to show that both human wisdom and the very testimony of our adversaries serve to support the Christian faith—a method which is not of recent introduction, but of established use, and has often been adopted by the holy Fathers of the Church. For instance, those venerable men, the witnesses and guardians of religious traditions, recognize a certain form and figure of this in the action of the Hebrews, who, when about to depart out of Egypt, were commanded to take with them the gold and silver vessels and precious robes of the Egyptians, that by a change of use the things might be dedicated to the service of the true God which had formerly been the instruments of ignoble and superstitious rites. Gregory of Neocaesarea[10] praises Origen expressly because, with singular dexterity, as one snatches weapons from the enemy, he turned to the defense of Christian wisdom and to the destruction of superstition many arguments drawn from the writings of the pagans. And both Gregory of Nazianzus[11] and Gregory of Nyssa[12] praise and commend a like mode of disputation in Basil the Great; while Jerome especially commends it in Quadratus, a disciple of the apostles, in Aristides, Justin, Irenaeus, and very many others.[13] Augustine says: "Do we not see Cyprian, that mildest of doctors and most blessed of martyrs, going out of Egypt laden with gold and silver and vestments? And Lactantius also and Victorinus, Optatus and Hilary? And, not to speak of the living, how many Greeks have done likewise?"[14] But if natural reason first sowed this rich field of doctrine before it was rendered fruitful by the power of Christ, it must assuredly become more prolific after the grace of the Savior has renewed and added to the native faculties of the human mind. And who does not see that a plain and easy road is opened up to faith by such a method of philosophic study?

But the advantage to be derived from such a school of philosophy is not to be confined within these limits. The foolishness of those men is gravely reproved in the words of divine wisdom who by these good things that are seen could not understand Him that is, neither by attending to the works could have acknowledged who was the workman.[15] In the first place, then, this great and noble fruit is gathered from human reason, that it demonstrates that God *is; for by the greatness of the beauty, and of the creature,* the *Creator of them may be seen so as to be known thereby.*[16] Again, it shows God to excel in the height of all perfections, in infinite wisdom before which nothing lies hidden, and in absolute justice which no depraved affection could possibly shake; and that God, therefore, is not only true but truth itself, which can neither deceive nor be deceived. Whence it clearly follows that human reason finds the fullest faith and authority united in the word of God. In like manner reason declares that the doctrine of the Gospel has even from its very beginning been made manifest by cer-

tain wonderful signs, the established proofs, as it were, of
unshaken truth; and that all, therefore, who set faith in the
Gospel do not believe rashly as though following cunning-
ly devised fables,[17] but, by a most reasonable consent, subject their intelligence and judgment to an authority which
is divine. And of no less importance is it that reason most
clearly sets forth that the Church instituted by Christ (as
laid down in the Vatican Synod), on account of its wonderful spread, its marvelous sanctity, and its inexhaustible
fecundity in all places, as well as of its Catholic unity and
unshaken stability, is in itself a great and perpetual motive
of belief and an irrefragable testimony of its own divine
mission.[18]

Its solid foundations having been thus laid, a perpetual
and varied service is further required of philosophy, in
order that sacred theology may receive and assume the
nature, form, and genius of a true science. For in this, the
most noble of studies, it is of the greatest necessity to bind
together, as it were, in one body the many and various parts
of the heavenly doctrines, that, each being allotted to its
own proper place and derived from its own proper principles, the whole may join together in a complete union; in
order, in fine, that all and each part may be strengthened by
its own and the others' invincible arguments. Nor is that
more accurate or fuller knowledge of the things that are
believed, and somewhat more lucid understanding, as far
as it can go, of the very mysteries of faith which Augustine
and the other Fathers commended and strove to reach, and
which the Vatican Synod itself[19] declared to be most fruitful, to be passed over in silence or belittled. Those will
certainly more fully and more easily attain that knowledge
and understanding who to integrity of life and love of faith
join a mind rounded and finished by philosophic studies, as
the same Vatican Synod teaches that the knowledge of such
sacred dogmas ought to be sought as well from analogy of

the things that are naturally known as from the connection of those mysteries one with another and with the final end of man.[20]

Lastly, the duty of religiously defending the truths divinely delivered, and of resisting those who dare oppose them, pertains to philosophic pursuits. Wherefore it is the glory of philosophy to be esteemed as the bulwark of faith and the strong defense of religion. As Clement of Alexandria testifies, the doctrine of the Savior is indeed perfect in itself and wants naught, since it is the power and wisdom of God. And the assistance of Greek philosophy makes not the truth more powerful; but in as much as it weakens the contrary arguments of the sophists and repels the veiled attacks against the truth, it has been fitly called the hedge and fence of the vine.[21] For as the enemies of the Catholic name, when about to attack religion, are in the habit of borrowing their weapons from the arguments of philosophers, so the defenders of sacred science draw many arguments from the store of philosophy which may serve to uphold revealed dogmas. Nor is the triumph of the Christian faith a small one in using human reason to repel powerfully and speedily the attacks of its adversaries by the hostile arms which human reason itself supplied. Which species of religious strife St. Jerome, writing to Magnus, notices as having been adopted by the Apostle of the Gentiles himself: Paul, the leader of the Christian army skillfully turns even a chance inscription into an argument for the faith; for he had learned from the true David to wrest the sword from the hands of the enemy and to cut off the head of the boastful Goliath with his own weapon.[22] Moreover, the Church herself not only urges, but even commands, Christian teachers to seek help from philosophy. For the fifth Council of the Lateran, after it had decided that "every assertion contrary to the truth of revealed faith is altogether false, for the reason that it contradicts, however slightly, the truth,"[23] advises teachers of philosophy to pay close attention to the exposition of fallacious arguments; since, as Augustine testifies, "if reason is turned against the authority of Sacred Scripture, no matter how specious it may seem, it errs in the likeness of truth; for true it cannot be."[24]

But in order that philosophy may be found equal to the gathering of those precious fruits which we have indicated, it behooves it above all things never to turn aside from that path which the Fathers have entered upon from a venerable antiquity, and which the Vatican Council solemnly and authoritatively approved. As it is evident that very many truths of the supernatural order which are far beyond the reach of the keenest intellect must be accepted, human reason, conscious of its own infirmity, dare not pretend to what is beyond it, nor deny those truths, nor measure them by its own standard, nor interpret them at will; but receive them rather with a full and humble faith, and esteem it the highest honor to be allowed to wait upon heavenly doctrines like a handmaid and attendant, and by God's goodness attain to them in any way whatsoever. But in the case of such doctrines as the human intelligence may perceive, it is equally just that philosophy should make use of its own method, principles, and arguments—not indeed in such fashion as to seem rashly to withdraw from the divine authority. But since it is established that those things which become known by revelation have the force of certain truth, and that those things which war against faith war equally against right reason, the Catholic philosopher will know that he violates at once faith and the laws of reason if he accepts any conclusion which he understands to be opposed to revealed doctrine.

We know that there are some who, in their overestimate of the human faculties, maintain that as soon as man's intellect becomes subject to divine authority it falls from its native dignity, and, hampered by the yoke of this species of slavery, is much retarded and hindered in its progress towards the supreme truth and excellence. Such an idea is most false and deceptive, and its final result is to induce foolish and ungrateful men willfully to repudiate the most sublime truths, and reject the divine gift of faith, from which the fountains of all good things flow out upon civil society. For the human mind, being confined within certain limits, and those narrow enough, is exposed to many errors and is ignorant of many things; whereas the Christian faith, reposing on the authority of God, is the unfailing mistress of truth, whom whoso follows he will be neither immeshed in the snares of error nor tossed hither and thither on the waves of fluctuating opinion. Those, therefore, who to the study of philosophy unite obedience to the Christian faith are philosophers indeed; for the splendor of the divine truths, received into the mind, helps the understanding, and not only detracts in nowise from its dignity, but adds greatly to its nobility, keenness, and stability. For surely that is a worthy and most useful exercise of reason when men give their minds to disproving those things which are repugnant to faith and proving the things which conform to faith. In the first case they cut the ground from under the feet of error and expose the viciousness of the arguments on which error rests; while in the second case they make themselves masters of weighty reasons for the sound demonstration of truth and the satisfactory instruction of any reasonable person. Whoever denies that such study and practice tend to add to the resources and expand the faculties of the mind must necessarily and absurdly hold that the mind gains nothing from discriminating between the true and the false. Justly, therefore, does the Vatican Council commemorate in these words the great benefits which faith has conferred upon reason: *Faith frees and saves reason from error, and endows it with manifold knowledge.*[25] A wise man, therefore, would not accuse faith and look upon it as opposed to reason and natural truths, but would rather offer heartfelt thanks to God, and sincerely rejoice that in the density of ignorance and in the flood-tide of error, holy faith, like a friendly star, shines down upon his path and points out to him the fair gate of truth beyond all danger of wandering.

If, venerable brethren, you open the history of philosophy, you will find all we have just said proved by experience. The philosophers of old who lacked the gift of faith, yet were esteemed so wise, fell into many appalling errors. You know how often among some truths they taught false and incongruous things; what vague and doubtful opinions they held concerning the nature of the Divinity, the first origin of things, the government of the world, the divine knowledge of the future, the cause and principle of evil, the ultimate end of man, eternal beatitude, concerning virtue and vice, and other matters, a true and certain knowledge of which is most necessary to the human race; while, on the other hand, the early Fathers and Doctors of the Church, who well understood that, according to the divine plan, the restorer of human science is Christ, who is the power and wisdom of God,[26] *and in whom are hidden all the treasures of wisdom and knowledge,*[27] took up and investigated the books of the ancient philosophers, and compared their teachings with the doctrines of revelation, and, carefully sifting them, they cherished what was true and wise in them and amended or rejected all else. For as the all-seeing God against the cruelty of tyrants raised up mighty martyrs to the defense of the Church, men prodigal of their great lives, in like manner to false philosophers and heretics He opposed men of great wisdom, to defend, even by the aid of human reason, the treasure of revealed truths. Thus from the very first ages of the Church, Catholic doctrine has encountered a multitude of most bitter adversaries, who, deriding the Christian dogmas and institutions, maintained that there were many gods, that the material world never had a beginning or cause, and that the course of events was one of blind and fatal necessity, not regulated by the will of divine Providence.

But the learned men whom we call apologists speedily encountered these teachers of foolish doctrine, and, under the guidance of faith, found arguments in human wisdom also to prove that one God, who stands pre-eminent in every kind of perfection, is to be worshiped; that all things were created from nothing by His omnipotent power; that by His wisdom they flourish and serve each their own special purposes. Among these St. Justin Martyr claims the chief place. After having tried the most celebrated academies of the Greeks, he saw clearly, as he himself confesses, that he could only draw truths in their fullness from the doctrines of revelation. These he embraced with all the ardor of his soul, purged of calumny, courageously and fully defended before the Roman emperors, and reconciled with them not a few of the sayings of the Greek philosophers.

Quadratus also and Aristides, Hermias and Athenagoras, stood nobly forth in that time. Nor did Irenaeus, the invincible martyr and bishop of Lyons, win less glory in the same cause when, forcibly refuting the perverse opinions of the Orientals, the work of the Gnostics, scattered broadcast over the territories of the Roman Empire, he explained (according to Jerome) the origin of each heresy and in what philosophic source it took its rise.[28] But who knows not the disputations of Clement of Alexandria, which the same Jerome thus honorably commemorates: "What is there in them that is not learned, and what that is not of the very heart of philosophy?"[29] He himself, indeed, with marvelous versatility treated of many things of the greatest utility for preparing a history of philosophy, for the exercise of the dialectic art, and for showing the agreement between reason and faith. After him came Origen, who graced the chair of the school of Alexandria, and was most learned in the teachings of the Greeks and Orientals. He published many volumes, involving great labor, which were wonderfully adapted to explain the divine writings and illustrate the sacred dogmas; which, though, as they now stand, not altogether free from error, contain nevertheless a wealth of knowledge tending to the growth and advance of natural truths. Tertullian opposes heretics with the authority of the sacred writings; with the philosophers he changes his defense and disputes philosophically; but so learnedly and accurately did he confute them that he made bold to say, "Neither in science nor in schooling are we equals, as you imagine."[30] Arnobius, also, in his works against the pagans, and Lactantius in the divine *Institutions* especially, with equal eloquence and strength strenuously strive to move men to accept the dogmas and precepts of Catholic wisdom, not by philosophic juggling, after the fashion of the academics, but vanquishing them partly by their own arms, and partly by arguments drawn from the mutual contentions of the philosophers.[31] But the writings on the human soul, the divine attributes, and other questions of mighty moment which the great Athanasius and Chrysostom, the prince of orators, have left behind them are, by common consent, so supremely excellent that it seems scarcely anything could be added to their subtlety and fullness. And, not to cover too wide a range, we add to the number of the great men of whom mention has been made the names of Basil the Great and of the two Gregories, who, on going forth from Athens, that home of all learning, thoroughly equipped with all the harness of philosophy, turned the wealth of knowledge which each had gathered up in a course of zealous study to the work of refuting heretics and preparing Christians.

But Augustine would seem to have wrested the palm from all. Of a most powerful genius and thoroughly saturated with sacred and profane learning, with the loftiest faith and with equal knowledge, he combated most vigorously all the errors of his age. What height of philosophy did he not reach? What region of it did he not diligently explore, either in expounding the loftiest mysteries of the faith to the faithful, or defending them against the fell onslaught of adversaries, or again when, in demolishing the fables of the academics or the Manichaeans, he laid the safe foundations and sure structure of human science, or followed up the reason, origin, and causes of the evils that afflict man? How subtly he reasoned on the angels, the soul, the human mind, the will and free choice, on religion and the life of the blessed, on time and eternity, and even on the very nature of changeable bodies! Afterwards, in the East, John Damascene, treading in the footsteps of Basil and of Gregory Nazianzen, and in the West Boethius and Anselm, following the doctrines of Augustine, added largely to the patrimony of philosophy.

Later on the doctors of the middle ages, who are called scholastics, addressed themselves to a great work—that of diligently collecting and sifting and storing up, as it were, in one place, for the use and convenience of posterity, the rich and fertile harvests of Christian learning scattered abroad in the voluminous works of the Holy Fathers. And with regard, venerable brethren, to the origin, drift, and excellence of this scholastic learning, it may be well here to speak more fully in the words of one of the wisest of our predecessors, Sixtus V: "By the divine favor of Him who alone gives the spirit of science, and wisdom, and understanding, and who through all ages, as there may be need, enriches His Church with new blessings and strengthens it with new safeguards, there was founded by our fathers, men of eminent wisdom, the scholastic theology, which two glorious doctors in par-

ticular, the angelic St. Thomas and the seraphic St. Bonaventure, illustrious teachers of this faculty,...with sur-
passing genius, by unwearied diligence, and at the cost of
long labors and vigils, set in order and beautified, and,
when skillfully arranged and clearly explained in a variety
of ways, handed down to posterity.

"And, indeed, the knowledge and use of so salutary a
science, which flows from the fertilizing founts of the sacred writings, the Sovereign Pontiffs, the Holy Fathers and
the councils, must always be of the greatest assistance to the
Church, whether with the view of really and soundly understanding and interpreting the Scriptures, or more safely
and to better purpose reading and explaining the Fathers,
or for exposing and refuting the various errors and heresies;
and in these late days, when those dangerous times described by the Apostle are already upon us, when the
blasphemers, the proud, and the seducers go from bad to
worse, erring themselves and causing others to err, there is
surely a very great need of confirming the dogmas of the
Catholic faith and confuting heresies."

Although these words seem to bear reference solely to
scholastic theology, nevertheless they may plainly be accepted as equally true of philosophy and its praises. For the
noble endowments which make the scholastic theology so
formidable to the enemies of truth—to wit, as the same
Pontiff adds, "that ready and close coherence of cause and
effect, that order and array as of a disciplined army in battle,
those clear definitions and distinctions, that strength of
argument and those keen discussions, by which light is
distinguished from darkness, the true from the false, expose and strip naked, as it were, the falsehoods of heretics
wrapped around by a cloud of subterfuges and fallacies"[32]—those noble and admirable endowments, we say,
are only to be found in a right use of that philosophy which
the scholastic teachers have been accustomed carefully and

prudently to make use of even in theological disputations. Moreover, since it is the proper and special office of the scholastic theologians to bind together by the fastest chain human and divine science, surely the theology in which they excelled would not have gained such honor and commendation among men if they had made use of a lame and imperfect or vain philosophy.

Among the scholastic doctors, the chief and master of all, towers Thomas Aquinas, who, as Cajetan observes, because "he most venerated the ancient doctors of the Church, in a certain way seems to have inherited the intellect of all."[33] The doctrines of those illustrious men, like the scattered members of a body, Thomas collected together and cemented, distributed in wonderful order, and so increased with important additions that he is rightly esteemed the special bulwark and glory of the Catholic faith. With his spirit at once humble and swift, his memory ready and tenacious, his life spotless throughout, a lover of truth for its own sake, richly endowed with human and divine science, like the sun he heated the world with the ardor of his virtues and filled it with the splendor of his teaching. Philosophy has no part which he did not touch finely at once and thoroughly; on the laws of reasoning, on God and incorporeal substances, on man and other sensible things, on human actions and their principles, he reasoned in such a manner that in him there is wanting neither a full array of questions, nor an apt disposal of the various parts, nor the best method of proceeding, nor soundness of principles or strength of argument, nor clearness and elegance of style, nor a facility for explaining what is abstruse.

Moreover, the Angelic Doctor pushed his philosophic conclusions into the reasons and principles of the things which are most comprehensive and contain in their bosom, so to say, the seeds of almost infinite truths, to be unfolded in good time by later masters and with a goodly yield. And as he also used this philosophic method in the refutation of error, he won this title to distinction for himself: that single-handed he victoriously combated the errors of former times, and supplied invincible arms to put those to rout which might in after-times spring up. Again, clearly distinguishing, as is fitting, reason from faith, while happily associating the one with the other, he both preserved the rights and had regard for the dignity of each; so much so, indeed, that reason, borne on the wings of Thomas to its human height, can scarcely rise higher, while faith could scarcely expect more or stronger aids from reason than those which she has already obtained through Thomas.

For these reasons learned men, in former ages especially, of the highest repute in theology and philosophy, after mastering with infinite pains the immortal works of Thomas, gave themselves up not so much to be instructed in his angelic wisdom as to be nourished upon it. It is known that nearly all the founders and framers of laws of the religious orders commanded their associates to study and religiously adhere to the teachings of St. Thomas, fearful lest any of them should swerve even in the slightest degree from the footsteps of so great a man. To say nothing of the family of St. Dominic, which rightly claims this great teacher for its own glory, the statutes of the Benedictines, the Carmelites, the Augustinians, the Society of Jesus, and many others, all testify that they are bound by this law.

And here how pleasantly one's thoughts fly back to those celebrated schools and academies which flourished of old in Europe, to Paris, Salamanca, Alcala, to Douay, Toulouse, and Louvain, to Padua and Bologna, to Naples and Coimbra, and to many another! All know how the fame of these seats of learning grew with their years, and that their judgment, often asked in matters of grave moment, held great weight everywhere. And we know how in those great homes of human wisdom, as in his own kingdom, Thomas reigned supreme; and that the minds of all, of teachers as well as of taught, rested in wonderful harmony under the shield and authority of the Angelic Doctor.

But, furthermore, our predecessors in the Roman pontificate have celebrated the wisdom of Thomas Aquinas by exceptional tributes of praise and the most ample testimonials. Clement VI in the Bull *In Ordine*, Nicholas V in his Brief to the Friars of the Order of Preachers, 1451, Benedict XIII in the Bull *Pretiosus*, and others bear witness that the universal Church borrows luster from his admirable teaching; while St. Pius V declares in the Bull *Mirabilis* that heresies, confounded and convicted by the same teaching, were dissipated, and the whole world daily freed from fatal errors; others, such as Clement XII in the Bull *Verbo Dei*, affirm that most fruitful blessings have spread abroad from his writings over the whole Church, and that he is worthy of the honor which is bestowed on the greatest doctors of the Church, on Gregory and Ambrose, Augustine and Jerome; while others have not hesitated to propose St. Thomas for the exemplar and master of the academies and great lyceums, whom they may follow with unfaltering feet. On which point the words of Blessed Urban V to the Academy of Toulouse are worthy to recall: "It is our will, which we hereby enjoin upon you, that you follow the teaching of Blessed Thomas as the true and Catholic doctrine, and that you labor with all your force to profit by the same."[34] Innocent XII in the Letter in the form of a Brief addressed on February 6, 1694, to the University of Louvain, followed the example of Urban in the case of the University of Louvain, and Benedict XIV in the Letter in the form of a Brief addressed on August 26, 1752, to the Dionysian College of Granada; while to these judgments of great Pontiffs on Thomas Aquinas comes the crowning testimony of Innocent VI: "His teaching above that of others, the canons alone excepted, enjoys such an elegance of phraseology, a method of statement, a truth of proposition, that those who hold to it are never found swerving from the path of truth, and he who dare assail it will always be suspected of error."[35]

The ecumenical councils also, where blossoms the flower of all earthly wisdom, have always been careful to hold Thomas Aquinas in singular honor. In the councils of Lyons, Vienne, Florence, and the Vatican one might almost say that Thomas took part and presided over the deliberations and decrees of the Fathers, contending against the errors of the Greeks, of heretics and rationalists, with invincible force and with the happiest results. But the chief and special glory of Thomas, one which he has shared with none of the Catholic doctors, is that the Fathers of Trent made it part of the order of the conclave to lay upon the altar, together with the code of Sacred Scripture and the decrees of the Supreme Pontiffs, the *Summa* of Thomas Aquinas, whence to seek counsel, reason, and inspiration.

A last triumph was reserved for this incomparable man— namely, to compel the homage, praise, and admiration of even the very enemies of the Catholic name. For it has come to light that there were not lacking among the leaders of heretical sects some who openly declared that, if the teaching of Thomas Aquinas were only taken away, they could easily battle with all Catholic teachers, gain the victory, and abolish the Church.[36] A vain hope indeed, but no vain testimony.

Therefore, venerable brethren, as often as we contemplate the good, the force, and the singular advantages to be derived from this system of philosophy which our Fathers so dearly loved, we think it hazardous that its special honor should not always and everywhere remain, especially when it is established that daily experience, and the judgment of the greatest men, and, to crown all, the voice of the Church, have favored the scholastic philosophy. Moreover, to the old teaching a novel system of philosophy has succeeded here and there, in which we fail to perceive those desirable and wholesome fruits which the Church and civil society itself would prefer. For it pleased the struggling innovators of the sixteenth century to philosophize without any respect for faith, the power of inventing in accordance with his own pleasure and bent being asked and given in turn by each one. Hence it was natural that systems of philosophy multiplied beyond measure, and conclusions differing and clashing one with another arose even about those matters which are the most important in human knowledge. From a mass of conclusions men often come to wavering and doubt; and who knows not how easily the mind slips from doubt to error? But as men are apt to follow the lead given them, this new pursuit seems to have caught the souls of certain Catholic philosophers, who, throwing aside the patrimony of ancient wisdom, chose rather to build up a new edifice than to strengthen and complete the old by the aid of the new—ill advisedly, in sooth, and not without detriment to the sciences. For a multiform system of this kind, which depends on the authority and choice of any professor, has a foundation open to change, and consequently gives us a philosophy not firm and stable and robust like that of old, but tottering and feeble. And if perchance it sometimes finds itself scarcely equal to sustain the shock of its foes, it should recognize that the cause and the blame lie in itself. In saying this we have no intention of discountenancing the learned and able men who bring their industry and erudition, and, what is more, the wealth of new discoveries, to the service of philosophy; for, of course, we understand that this tends to the development of learning. But one should be very careful lest all or his chief labor be exhausted in these pursuits and in mere erudition. And the same thing is true of sacred theology, which, indeed, may be assisted and illustrated by all kinds of erudition, though it is absolutely necessary to approach it in the grave manner of the scholastics, in order that, the forces of revelation and reason being united in it, it may continue to be "the invincible bulwark of the faith."[37]

With wise forethought, therefore, not a few of the advocates of philosophical studies, when turning their minds recently to the practical reform of philosophy, aimed and aim at restoring the renowned teaching of Thomas Aquinas and winning it back to its ancient beauty.

We have learned with great joy that many members of your order, venerable brethren, have taken this plan to heart; and while we earnestly commend their efforts, we exhort them to hold fast to their purpose, and remind each and all of you that our first and most cherished idea is that you should all furnish a generous and copious supply to studious youth of those crystal rills of wisdom flowing in a never-ending and fertilizing stream from the fountainhead of the Angelic Doctor.

Many are the reasons why we are so desirous of this. In the first place, then, since in the tempest that is on us the Christian faith is being constantly assailed by the machinations and craft of a certain false wisdom, all youths, but especially those who are the growing hope of the Church, should be nourished on the strong and robust food of doctrine, that so, mighty in strength and armed at all points, they may become habituated to advance the cause of religion with force and judgment, *being ready always*, according to the apostolic counsel, *to satisfy every one that asks you a reason of that hope which is in you*,[38] and that they may be able to exhort in sound doctrine and to convince the gainsayers.[39] Many of those who, with minds alienated from the faith, hate Catholic institutions, claim reason as their sole mistress and guide. Now, we think that, apart from the supernatural help of God, nothing is better calculated to heal those minds and to bring them into favor with the Catholic faith than the solid doctrine of the Fathers and the scholastics, who so clearly and forcibly demonstrate the firm foundations of the faith, its divine origin, its certain truth, the arguments that sustain it, the benefits it has conferred on the human race, and its perfect accord with reason, in a manner to satisfy completely minds open to persuasion, however unwilling and repugnant.

Domestic and civil society even, which, as all see, is exposed to great danger from this plague of perverse opinions, would certainly enjoy a far more peaceful and secure existence if a more wholesome doctrine were taught in the academies and schools—one more in conformity with the teaching of the Church, such as is contained in the works of Thomas Aquinas.

For the teachings of Thomas on the true meaning of liberty, which at this time is running into license, on the divine origin of all authority, on laws and their force, on the paternal and just rule of princes, on obedience to the higher powers, on mutual charity one towards another—on all of these and kindred subjects have very great and invincible force to overturn those principles of the new order which are well known to be dangerous to the peaceful order of things and to public safety. In short, all studies ought to find hope of advancement and promise of assistance in this restoration of philosophic discipline which we have proposed. The arts were wont to draw from philosophy, as from a wise mistress, sound judgment and right method, and from it also their spirit as from the common fount of life. When philosophy stood stainless in honor and wise in judgment, then, as facts and constant experience showed, the liberal arts flourished as never before or since; but, neglected and almost blotted out, they lay prone since philosophy began to lean to error and join hands with folly. Nor will the physical sciences, which are now in such great repute, and by the renown of so many inventions draw such universal admiration to themselves, suffer detriment but find very great assistance in the re-establishment of the ancient philosophy. For the investigation of facts and the contemplation of nature is not alone sufficient for their profitable exercise and advance; but when facts have been established it is necessary to rise and apply ourselves to the study of the nature of corporeal things, to inquire into the laws which govern them and the principles whence their order and varied unity and mutual attraction in diversity arise. To such investigations it is wonderful what force and light and aid the scholastic philosophy, if judiciously taught, would bring.

And here it is well to note that our philosophy can only by the grossest injustice be accused of being opposed to the advance and development of natural science. For when the scholastics, following the opinion of the holy Fathers, always held in anthropology that the human intelligence is led to the knowledge of things without body and matter only by things sensible, they readily understood that nothing was of greater use to the philosopher than diligently to search into the mysteries of nature and to be devoted with assiduous patience to the study of physical things. And this they confirmed by their own example; for St. Thomas, Blessed Albertus Magnus, and other leaders of the scholastics were never so wholly rapt in the study of philosophy as not to give large attention to the knowledge of natural things; and, indeed, the number of their sayings and writings on these subjects, which recent professors approve of and admit to harmonize with truth, is by no means small. Moreover, in this very age many illustrious professors of the physical sciences openly testify that between certain and accepted conclusions of modern physics and the philosophic principles of the schools there is no conflict worthy of the name.

While, therefore, we hold that every word of wisdom,

every useful thing by whomsoever discovered or planned, ought to be received with a willing and grateful mind, we exhort you, venerable brethren, in all earnestness to restore the golden wisdom of St. Thomas, and to spread it far and wide for the defense and beauty of the Catholic faith, for the good of society, and for the advantage of all the sciences. The wisdom of St. Thomas, we say; for if anything is taken up with too great subtlety by the scholastic doctors, or too carelessly stated—if there be anything that ill agrees with the discoveries of a later age, or, in a word, improbable in whatever way, it does not enter our mind to propose that for imitation to our age. Let carefully selected teachers endeavor to implant the doctrine of Thomas Aquinas in the minds of the students, and set forth clearly his solidity and excellence over others. Let the academies already founded or to be founded by you illustrate and defend this doctrine, and use it for the refutation of prevailing errors. But, lest the false for the true, or the corrupt for the pure be drunk in, be watchful that the doctrine of Thomas be drawn from his own fountains, or at least from those rivulets which, derived from the very fount, have thus far flowed, according to the established agreement of learned men, pure and clear; be careful to guard the minds of youth from those which are said to flow thence, but in reality are gathered from strange and unwholesome streams.

But well do we know that vain will be our efforts unless, venerable brethren, He helps our common cause who, in the words of divine Scripture, is called the God of all knowledge[40]; by which we are also admonished that *every best gift and every perfect gift is from above, coming down from the Father of lights*[41]; and again: *If any of you want wisdom, let him ask of God, who gives to all men abundantly, and upbraids not; and it shall be given him.*[42]

Therefore in this also let us follow the example of the Angelic Doctor, who never gave himself to reading or writing without first begging the blessing of God; who modestly confessed that whatever he knew he had acquired not so much by his own study and labor as by the divine gift. And therefore let us all, in humble and united prayer, beseech God to send forth the spirit of knowledge and of understanding to the children of the Church, and open their senses for the understanding of wisdom. And that we may receive fuller fruits of the divine goodness, offer up to God the most efficacious patronage of the Blessed Virgin Mary, who is called the seat of wisdom; having at the same time as advocates St. Joseph, the most chaste spouse of the Virgin, and Peter and Paul, the chiefs of the apostles, whose truth renewed the earth, which had fallen under the impure blight of error, filling it with the light of heavenly wisdom.

In fine, relying on the divine assistance and confiding in your pastoral zeal, we bestow on all of you, venerable brethren, on all the clergy and the flocks committed to your charge, the apostolic benediction as a pledge of heavenly gifts and a token of our special esteem.

1. Matthew 28:19.
2. Colossians 2:8.
3. 1 Corinthians 2:4.
4. *De Trin.*, xiv, I, 3 (PL 42, 1037).
5. Clem. Alex., *Strom.*, I, 16; VII, 3 (PG 8, 795; 9, 426).
6. Origen, *Epistola ad Gregorium* (PG 11, 87-91).
7. Clem. Alex., *Strom.*, I, 5 (PG 8, 718-719).
8. Romans 1:20.
9. *Ibid.*, 2:14, 15.
10. *Orat. paneg. ad Origen*, 14 (PG 10, 1094).
11. *Carm.* i, Iamb. 3.
12. *Vita Moysis* (PG 44, 359).
13. *Epist. ad Magnum*, 4 (PL 22, 667).
14. *De Doctr. Christ.*, I, ii, 40 (PL 34, 63).
15. Wisdom 13:1.
16. *Ibid.*, 13:5.
17. 2 Peter 1:16.

18. *Const. Dogm. de Fid. Cath.*, c. 3.

19. *Const. cit.*, c. 4.

20. *Loc. cit.*

21. *Strom.*, I, 20 (PG 8, 818).

22. *Epist. ad Magnum*, 2 (PL 22, 666).

23. Bulla *Apostolici regiminis*.

24. *Epist. 143 (al. 7), ad Marcelin.*, 7 (PL 33, 589).

25. *Const. Dogm. de Fid. Cath.*, c. 4.

26. 1 Corinthians 1:24.

27. Colossians 2:3.

28. *Epist. ad Magnum*, 4 (PL 22, 667).

29. *Loc. cit.*

30. *Apologet*, 46 (PL 1, 573).

31. *Inst.* vii, 7 (PL 6, 759).

32. Bulla *Triumphantis* an. 1588.

33. *In 2m., 2ae.*, q. 148, a. 4; Leonine ed. Vol. X, n. 6, p. 174.

34. *Const.* 5a. dat. die Aug. 3, 1368 ad Concell. Univ. Tolo.

35. *Serm. de S. Thoma.*

36. Bucer.

37. Sixtus V. Bulla *Triumphantis.*

38. 1 Peter 3:15.

39. Tit. 1:9.

40. 1 Kings 2:3.

41. Jas. 1:17.

42. Jas. 1:5.

INDEX